D1321034

Armoured Odyssey

ARMOURED ODYSSEY

8th Royal Tank Regiment in
The Western Desert 1941-1942
Palestine, Syria, Egypt 1943-1944
Italy 1944-1945

Stuart Hamilton MC

Introduction by Major-General H. M. Liardet
CB CBE DSO DL

Tom Donovan
London

First published in 1995 by

Tom Donovan Publishing Ltd.
52 Willow Road
Hampstead
London NW3 1TP

ISBN: 1-871085-30-6

Desk-top typeset by Tom Donovan Publishing Ltd.

Printed by The Bath Press, Bath

Contents

Maps

Illustrations

Forty-three photographs will be found between pages 82-83. All photographs are from the author's own collection, with the exceptions of numbers 6, 23, 24, 25, 26, 30, and 31, which are reproduced by kind permission of the Trustees of the Imperial War Museum, London, and number 38, which is reproduced by kind permission of the Tank Museum, Bovington Camp, Dorset. Maps 1-7 are reproduced from Captain Sir Basil Liddell Hart's *The Tanks* (Cassell, 1959)

Plates

1. 8th RTR Battle Flag. In fact a German ground-to-air recognition flag - scarlet with black swastika on white background - captured at Bardia 31st December 1941. The Germans would place this in front of their positions so that they would not be bombed by the Luftwaffe, as recognition was very difficult in the desert (we were bombed by the Desert Air Force on one occasion and twice we saw, to our great delight, Stuka dive bombers hit their own troops).

The five columns to the right of the swastika are the names of the officers who served with the 8th RTR. The first column and the first eight names in the second column are the 'originals' who left England in April 1941.

The two columns on the left of the swastika are the battle honours won in the Desert and in Italy.

The flag is now in the Tank Museum at Bovington.

2. Fort Capuzzo, November 1941. 'B' Squadron's first battle (with the New Zealand Division).

3. Sidi Rezegh 1941. Knocked-out in my first tank battle. My gunner unfortunately killed.

4. Sidi Rezegh Tomb, November 1941. Very heavy fighting here. Note German graves in foreground.

5. Sidi Rezegh, November 1941. "Three left out of 13" after the first week of the six-and-a-half week campaign: L-R, Reggie Campbell MC (wounded and burnt); Hickey Sugden MC & bar (twice wounded); Self ("a slight scratch"). Background: Tony Reid, Recce Officer, killed at Bardia, December 1941.

6. German Panzer Mark III. Knocked-out in Sidi Rezegh area. A good tank with a 50mm gun and two MGs, with a five man crew.

7. Tobruk outskirts, 1941. Handing over our Valentines - just seven left out of 52. Note hit on turret of leading tank. Mine is fifth or sixth, still with holes in turret.

8. 'C' Squadron, November/December 1941. L-R, Hickey Sugden MC &

bar; Peter Kitto; Tony Reid; Bertie Keelan; Ian Taylor. Peter, Tony and Ian killed: Bertie wounded.

9. Bardia, December 1941. Turret of Matilda tank captured and concreted into ground and used as an armoured pill-box. About 4 inches of armour: very difficult to knock out.

10. Our tanks before Bardia attack: bunched-up for propaganda photograph. The white-red-white identification stripes were soon covered with oil and sand as they proved too easy an aiming point for the Germans.

11, 12 & 13. German 88mm knocked out by Hickey Sugden, who stalked it after it had killed his friend Tony Reid. Note 2-pdr shell holes in gun shield. Hickey Sugden and Tony Reid.

14. 'B' Squadron, January/February 1942, Benghazi area. L-R, Reggie Campbell; Mike Hunt; Peter Butt; Leo Stock; self. Mike, Peter and Leo killed. Mike recommended for a posthumous VC at Alamein, but did not get it.

15. My tank en route for Benghazi, early January 1942. Very cold wind hence leather jerkin, gloves etc.

16. "HAM-BROS!" El Adem, February 1942. Self with elder brother Gerald (Captain, RASC), who turned up with a crate of beer.

17. March/April 1942. Douglas Dawson, Charles 'Batty' Attwood, Leslie 'Doc' Milton, George Sutton.

18. Our tanks disguised, using "sunshields," as lorries, whilst on a raid behind enemy lines during the 'Pimple' attack. We are in a rather large 'Deir' - or depression - in the desert.

19. Bliss! Sunset in the desert, April/May 1942.

20. Tamar area May/June 1942. Different types os desert terrain showing thorny scrub and loose sandy pebbles. Tank tracks in foreground. Heavy tank battles here during this period. Vehicles on horizon - "Whose? Theirs or Ours?" "Don't know old boy - you'd better go and have a 'shufti'."

21. Knightsbridge area, May/June 1942. Hard, stony ground littered with small rocks. Hellish going for trucks, particularly ambulances with wounded. Eventually known as The Cauldron, and the scene of heavy fighting, 8th Army losing a big tank battle. Believe it or not the thin black line in the foreground is a Bedouin Arab with his flock of goats.

22. Khamsin sandstorm approaching, June 1942. Could last for two days like this. Absolute misery and heat unbearable.

23. German Panzer Mark IV 'Special' with long-barrelled 75mm firing a 15lb shell. Damn good tank.

24. The Cauldron, June 1942. A quick breather before attacking. Believe they are 4th RTR Valentines. Apparently their white-red-white identification stripes have been erased.

25 & 26. Tank battle casualties. Extricating a wounded map (top) and Military Police extricating a corpse, headless and charred (bottom).

27. Alamein, July 1942. Self; Reggie Campbell; unknown replacement officer killed the next day. Very, very tired. Dessert sores on nose, hands and legs.

28. Reggie at Alamein, July 1942. Utter exhaustion.

29. Alamein, July 1942. Self in centre wearing sun glasses. Pipe in stocking top - never without it! After being told, yet again, that we were being pulled out we were then told to mount a dawn attack the next day - with the Aussies - at Tel El Eisa (the Hill of Jesus).

30. Alamein, October 1942. German Mark IV dug-in near Raham Track.

31. Alamein, October 1942. "The hammering of the Panzers."

32. Bill Fairclough MC. Killed at Alamein October 1942 after being knocked-out of three tanks on three successive days.

33. Doc Leslie Milton. A very popular and well-liked man.

34. Padre Sam Kemble. Equally liked and popular with all in the Regiment.

35. Tel Aviv, Palestine 1943. Self and John Herbertson MBE on leave, my finger fractured playing rugger.

36. My Sherman tank "Hornbill" and crew, Fayid area, Egypt 1944. L-R, Eric Mace (lap gunner); L/Cpl Stanley Shapcott (75mm gunner); L/Cpl Tim Clayton (driver - killed in Gothic Line); 'Curly' Carter (wireless operator - bald as a coot!)

37. Self with "Hornbill."

38. Citta St. Angelo, Italy, May 1944. Captain John Robinson MC and Major Peter Butt receiving two flags from Mayor and ladies who had secretly made them (see text). Now in Tank Museum at Bovington.

39. Croce 1944. Knocked-out Shermans. Bitter fighting here.

40. Monte Gemmano 1944. Heavy machine-gunners firing on the town.

41. Gothic Line 1944. Knocked-out German S/P gun. 155mm?

42. 8th RTR Squadron Commanders, July 1944. L-R, Self; Reggie Campbell MC; Tom Hendrie DSO; Hickey Sugden MC & bar. Self, Reggie and Hickey were the "three originals." Reggie and Tom died after the war.

43. Self just before final battle, April 9th, 1944.

Acknowledgements

To my daughter Fiona, for her patient and endless long hours of typing and re-typing; to her husband Peter, for his splendid effort in putting this manuscript together so well.

To Bill Green for his great help with the lists of awards, decorations and Roll of Honour; to David Fletcher, the Librarian at the Tank Museum at Bovington Camp, in allowing me to spend several days there checking through the 8th RTR War Diary and the various memorabilia available.

To Lt. Col. Gordon K. Defrates DSO MC and bar, who introduced me to Paul Riches, whose interest and enthusiasm finally persuaded Tom Donovan to publish these memoirs.

To you all, my very grateful thanks as without your interest, help and assistance this could never have happened.

Foreword

I have been asked why, after a lapse of some 50 years, I have written these memoirs.

There are two reasons, the first of which is that the War Diary for the greater part of the Western Desert Campaign unfortunately was lost and so there is no record of how the 8th RTR operated during the critical periods of 1942, and there appears to be only a very scrappy account of the Regiment's operations in the Tank Museum in Bovington Camp.

However, the main reason is that I feel that somewhere there needs to be a record of what it was like to be a member of a tank crew in the heat and dust of battle in the Western Desert, and also what it was like to be a tank man in the arduous conditions imposed by the terrain, fighting in Italy.

The extraordinary courage, sheer guts and the stoic endurance the ordinary 'tankie' showed throughout both campaigns never ceased to amaze me. No matter how bad the conditions no-one ever failed to do his job - more than just his job in many cases - and no-one ever queried an order or shirked doing it, even when it appeared dangerous and at times almost damn' suicidal.

It is for these reasons that these memoirs have been written and I think that it is only right that future historians and possibly distant relatives should know the splendid job such men as these carried out, and they should feel proud and grateful for what these men did and went through.

I too feel very proud to have known such fine men and have had the privilege to be associated with them.

As these notes are being typed some 50 years late with the aid of only sketchy old diaries and old maps it is possible that some dates and place names may be slightly inaccurate and out of chronological sequence.

However, the people mentioned and the events described were very real and very definitely happened. Some of the incidents may appear to be some what exaggerated and a little far-fetched, but I can assure readers that they did happen exactly as described and the old saying 'truth is stranger than fiction' is very apt in wartime.

Stuart Hamilton, 1995

Glossary

Alam	Cairn
Bir	Rock cistern or well
Deir	Depression
Ghot	Area cultivated after rain
Haqfet	Open or ruined cistern
Hatiya	Patch of scrub
Minqar	Promontory on land
Qabr	Grave
Ras	Headland
Sabakha	Dry salt marsh
Sidi	Tomb or grave
Sanyet	Deep well
Tallet	Hill
Wadi	Watercourse; usually dried up

Introduction

by

Major-General H.M. Liardet CB CBE DSO DL

I commanded the 8th Royal Tank Regiment shortly after the Second World War ended. Consequently I felt very pleased and honoured when I was asked by Stuart Hamilton to write a short introduction to this book.

I am always very proud to have served in the 8th RTR, albeit in peacetime, but I was always very conscious of the splendid wartime service the Regiment had given and did my best to further this spirit in the Regiment.

'Armoured Odyssey' fills in a very important hole in the history of tank warfare. It is one of the very few books written which gives the real feel of a tank crew in battle. When you read it, you know what it was like: the atmosphere of tension, the smell of cordite and diesel fuel, the dust, the continuous babble of the wireless, the crack of the 2-pounder gun, the rattle of the Besa machine-gun!

The fear and the humour, the apprehension and the relief, the sadness at the loss of a good comrade and above all, transcending all, the utter fatigue of battle.

All through the Desert war, and later in the very different Italian Campaign, Hamilton makes the situation absolutely clear and always interesting.

This book will be very much enjoyed by old tank soldiers who will remember what they went through in the war years. It will also be of great interest to the many of today's public who study and research the history of the Second World War.

In my opinion it is an outstanding contribution to history, and as such, I strongly recommend it to the interested public.

1
The Western Desert 1941-1942

It is just as well that I am not superstitious because when I left the 5th RTR to go to the OCTU in January 1940 I was posted to 13 Troop and on July 13th just 13 of us were duly commissioned. When the 8th RTR left the UK in April 1941 to go out to the Middle East our serial number was 175, which of course adds up to 13, and we disembarked at Suez on June 13th. When we first went into action in November 1941, to relieve Tobruk, we were attached to 13 Corps and we went in only 13 Troop Officers strong, instead of 15, and at the end of the first week of that six-and-a-half weeks campaign there were just three of us left. By the fortunes of war we all three survived and were together in Italy - each commanding our own Squadrons - at the end of the war on May 2nd 1945. So from then onwards 13 was my lucky number.

On being commissioned in July 1940 I was posted to the Brigade Headquarters of the lst Army Tank Brigade (Heavy Tanks) then under the command of Brigadier H.R.B. Watkins DSO - known as 'Boomer.'

Whilst the work was quite interesting as the Troop Officer in command of the Brigade HQ Tanks, which then consisted of three Vickers Light Tanks, and I had a lot to do (and learn), it was not really to my liking and to my great delight in November of that year I was posted to the 8th RTR who were then down in Barham, Kent. They were a regular Battalion of the Royal Tank Regiment and I joined 'B' Squadron commanded by Major George Sutton MC. He went on to be awarded a DSO and a bar to his MC in 1941/1942.

I was even more fortunate to remain with them for the whole of the war and when it ended I was one of the three originals left out of all those who had left the UK in 1941.

We were equipped with the Matilda Infantry Tank, a very fine tank at that stage of the war, and our Brigade, which consisted of the 8th, the 42nd, and the 44th RTR, was about the only fully equipped Brigade in England after the debacle of Dunkirk and as such we were down in the South East corner for anti-invasion and anti-parachute duties.

I was married on April 10th 1941 and had just five days with my wife before being shipped overseas and I didn't see her again for four years and two months, which was some way to start one's marriage.

We left England in April 1941 on the Polish ship SS *Sobieski* and had a fairly uneventful voyage except for a submarine scare off the west coast of Africa and a ferocious storm, which I believe was of hurricane velocity, going round the Cape, and I understand that something like six people were washed overboard in the convoy. Being typically British we did lots of exercises in the heat and of course had the finals of the tug-of-war going up the Red Sea, which just about prostrated everybody, spectators as well.

We disembarked at Suez on June 13th and proceeded to a base camp at Sidi Bishr, just outside Alexandria. Unfortunately the convoy with our Matilda tanks, which went through the Mediterranean, was very badly hit and most of our tanks sunk and what few came through were immediately handed out to the 4th and 7th RTR, then fighting a pretty desperate but pretty hopeless battle called 'Battle-Axe' in the desert.

We tried to get ourselves acclimatised to the heat, and working parties were sent down to tank base workshops in Alexandria to help out. They were shattered to find tanks, which had been picked up on the battlefields and brought straight back to workshops for repair, burnt and with nasty looking holes in them. As they had been picked up very quickly, where knocked out, some even had the remains of their crews inside.

This was not a good psychological move for us at all and we were told that the damage was done by a deadly German gun called an 88mm. This was the famous, or rather infamous, German 88mm anti-aircraft gun, now being used in an anti-tank role, and it had a devastating effect on tanks in the desert as it could knock out anything we had at a range of 3000 yards or more.

In retrospect, if only we had used our excellent 3.7 inch ack-ack gun in a similar role what a hell of a difference this would have made in the desert battles on the flat, open and wide areas, but the Powers-that-be unfortunately thought otherwise, if they thought at all. I believe that one of the fatuous reasons given for not using it was because of its height off the ground, thus giving no protection to its crews, also its height would make it an easy target. Just look at a photograph of an 88mm...

We were then equipped with a brand new tank called a Valentine. This was small with a low silhouette, had only a three man crew but was heavily armoured, being about three-and-a-half inches thick, but most unfortunately armed with a piddling little 2-pounder pop-gun and a Besa machine-gun. A three man crew was an awful disadvantage as the wretched tank commander had not only to command the tank and his Troop, or Squadron, but also had to load both the guns and work the wireless set as well and when things got hectic in a battle, then life was very hectic indeed.

The 2-pdr had been effective in close quarter fighting as in 1940 in France but now, 18 months later, on the flat, wide, open desert well, frankly, it was bloody useless because the German Panzer Mark III with its 50 millimetre and the Panzer Mark IV with its 75 millimetre could out-gun us all the time, being able to knock us out at 900/1000 yards range, let alone the 88mms at 3000 yards. As we could only knock them out at about 400/500 yards it was really like being a lightweight in the ring with a heavyweight. The German tanks also had five man crews and they were faster than ours as they could do about 20-25 mph, whereas we could only manage 15-20 mph. The one thing that was in our favour was that our armour was thicker, and as we were diesel tanks and not petrol we did not brew up as quickly when hit.

The desert was nothing like what one had expected. No golden sand with soft billowy sand-dunes and palm trees and all that sort of rubbish à la Hollywood - the Western Desert was really a flat rocky plateau stretching for hundreds of miles west from Alexandria in Egypt, through into Cyrenaica, to Tripolitania and probably up into Tunisia as well. Right on the edge of the coast, where the rain fell several times a year, there were a few pieces of greenery round about such places as Mersa Matruh, Sidi Barani and Tobruk. Also of course the lovely green, fertile area of Northern Libya around Derna, Barce and Benghazi, but the rest of it was this huge, flat, rocky plateau covered with this loose dirty sand, stones and small rocks.

Where the escarpment did reach the coast it could descend very steeply and rapidly as around about Sollum and Halfaya Pass (naturally named Hellfire Pass) and at Bardia and Tobruk where there were great rocky ravines and wadis. Again, in Northern Libya around Cirene and Barce were the Jebel mountains.

When I said that the desert was flat there were of course undulations in the ground, sometimes quite shallow which could be filled with soft sand and could catch an unwary vehicle and get it bogged, and some of the deeper depressions, called Deirs, could hold 20 or 30 vehicles or more, but generally speaking it was flat and there was absolutely no cover for tanks or vehicles to use to hide themselves.

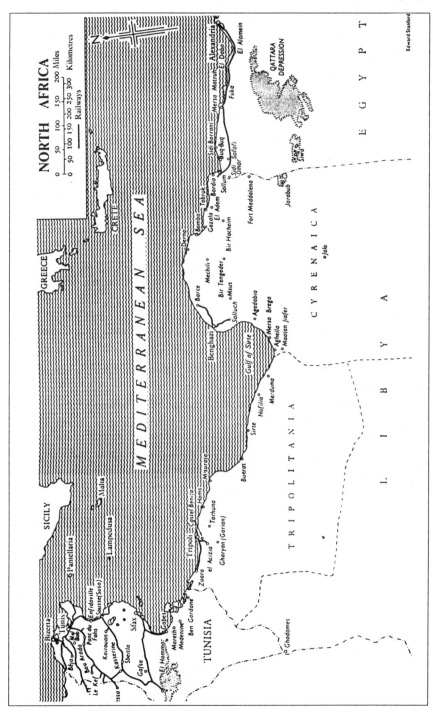

Really the desert battles were I suppose rather like a sea battle - a question of manoeuvrability. One had to use one's own skill and initiative to outmanoeuvre the enemy and hit him in the flank. When I talk of hundreds of miles I mean exactly that because in those days, in 1941, railhead was at Mersa Matruh about 250 miles or so from Alexandria, and Tobruk was a further 300 miles and Benghazi was another 320 miles on. So when we were up south and west of Benghazi we were literally 1000 miles from base at Alexandria. The problem of supply and logistics was therefore absolutely nightmarish. When you think of how one soldier or one tank was supplied over these vast distances with food, water, fuel, ammunition, spares and clothing, well the mind just boggles. This was done by setting up vast dumps away from railhead the further we advanced west: of course these dumps had to be maintained and protected so the wastage of man power was again considerable.

I mentioned earlier in this narrative that when I was posted to the 8th RTR in November 1940 I joined 'B' Squadron under George Sutton, and what a tremendous character he was. To us he was an old man because he was then probably about 43 and we were all about 20 years younger. He had scraped into World War One where he was awarded an MC as a subaltern with the Rifle Brigade fighting in the trenches. He then became a rubber planter out in Malaya and his stories about that part of the world at that time were simply hair-raising. He was the complete and typical Somerset Maugham type of character.

He was also at one time a King's Messenger - which I believe is rather a special distinction - and at the outbreak of war he immediately volunteered and to his disgust was placed, because of his age, into the Pioneer Corps. He went over to France in 1939/40 and because of his fluent Dutch he swanned around in Holland and Belgium doing some sort of intelligence work - for which effort he was on the Gestapo's wanted list.

He got back to Calais when the debacle started and with a Guards sergeant he stood on a road, with his pistol in his hand, stopped every single soldier who had a rifle and ordered them into fields and to start digging trenches. In this way he collected over 200 men to help in the defence of Calais. He was one of the very last to leave, literally jumping onto the decks of a destroyer as it was leaving the docks.

When he got back to England he met our Brigadier, 'Boomer' Watkins somewhere who was so impressed with him that he got him out of the Pioneer Corps and transferred to the RTR and had him posted to the 8th Tanks.

In the eight months from November 1941 to June 1942 George won a bar to his MC and the DSO as well and his portrait was painted by one of the official War Artists. He went back to the UK early in 1943 because he very badly damaged his hand in a tank battle when, in typical George manner, he dropped his microphone into the chute bag to catch the empty shell cases and as he put his hand down to retrieve it the gunner fired and smashed his arm. He eventually ended up as a lieutenant-colonel commanding a Prisoner of War camp in England and when I met him after the War he gleefully told me the first thing he did was to shake everything up, and by that he meant he started on the prison staff, insisting that every able bodied man was sacked and sent back to a fighting unit and then he said, with another gleam in his eye, he got cracking on the bloody Jerries.

He confessed he knew very little about administration, as that he said was for his second in command and his Sergeant-Major, but as regards fighting, well that was quite a different matter. He had the extraordinary axiom that the safest place to be in any battle or scrap was right in the thick of it, as in his opinion everybody was too busy shooting at everybody else to shoot at him. As a result of this I stuck to him like a leech and managed to survive, yet on two separate occasions in the desert I was at hand when the 'silly old bugger' - as we affectionately called him - got himself knocked out, and I was able to pick him up both times.

The men would follow him anywhere as he was very much loved and respected and I am glad to say he reached the ripe old age of 80 before he died, being cheerful right to the very end, truly a magnificent character, and one quite irreplaceable.

In July/August we moved well and truly up into The Blue to get ourselves properly acclimatised to desert conditions and desert living, ie: the heat, the sun, the dust, the flies and of course getting used to our new Valentine tanks.

We were all very keen and knew that something was in the air. Life seemed pretty good to me at that time until I started to feel very peculiar and act in a very odd way and it was diagnosed that I had jaundice, so I was packed off on a train back to Alexandria. I went absolutely as yellow as a Chinaman and after about two weeks in hospital I was sent off on a convalescence, but on about the second or third day I met one of the Squadron NCOs who told me with great excitement that we had moved very much closer up to The Wire and that things were hotting up generally.

The Wire was literally a fence of barbed wire about eight feet high and 12 feet thick stretching from Sollum on the coast southwards to Jarabub, about 200 miles, and was the frontier wire erected by the Italians to demark the frontier between Egypt and Cyrenaica. He also informed me, to my horror, that a new officer had taken over my Troop and that he wasn't liked at all because he had very weird ideas.

I therefore discharged myself immediately and had a hell of a party that night and nearly collapsed on the train going back up to my unit because no-one had told me that having had jaundice I shouldn't have any alcohol for about three months. I received a good welcome from the Squadron and my Troop in particular and the new officer was sent packing.

In September 1941 the old Western Desert force had been so reinforced and re-equipped that it was henceforth to be known as the 8th Army. First Army Tank Brigade, consisting of the 8th, 42nd and 44th RTR, was part of 13 Corps and we the 8th RTR were attached to the New Zealand Division. These were magnificent seasoned fighting troops with whom we were very proud to be associated and we got down to liaising strongly for future operations.

We had moved up even closer to The Wire and it was really a magnificent sight to see the whole of the New Zealand Division and ourselves spread out across the desert because wherever one looked in any direction there were tanks, guns, trucks, lorries, artillery, anti-tank guns, ack-ack guns and so on. Everything one could imagine on the move.

During one of our halts some of the New Zealand officers came over to inspect our tanks and I was with one whilst Sgt. George, later to win a fine DCM, was explaining to the two Kiwi officers inside the turret how everything worked. One of them, sitting in the gunner's seat said, "What happens if I squeeze this?" and of course he did and to everybody's horror the 2-pdr gun fired and the shell went screaming through this mass of transport, disappearing out of sight, but, thank God! without hitting anything! The other officer turned round and looked up at Sgt. George and grinned wryly, saying, "I hope you can shoot fucking better than that mate!"

On the afternoon of November 19th 1941 we had orders that we were going to cross The Wire into Libya, at night, and there was the most tremendous excitement all round as we were all keyed up and ready to go.

The sun was setting rapidly in the west in a great red orb when a truck came roaring up to me, creating a great cloud of dust, and our Intelligence Officer, Charles 'Batty' Attwood bellowed out from the top that we were to move off immediately on a bearing of 278 degrees, roughly due west, for about six miles somewhere over there. "There will be a light on the top of a staff car" he yelled, being in a tremendous flap, as he shot off in the gloom, not giving me a chance to confirm his instructions. I went and reported to George what Charles had said and he looked at me and smiled saying, "OK Ham! As you have heard the orders you can lead us off." I was absolutely horrified because I wasn't really certain if I had heard, and understood, just exactly what Charles was saying, but off we moved. I was sweating like hell because there were scores of vehicles on the move, dust everywhere, the sky had clouded over, the sun had set and I was frantically stopping my tank, getting out and taking a compass bearing, getting inside again and checking with my driver how far we had gone and after about five or six miles we seemed to be absolutely nowhere.

I was in a terrible panic because I was utterly and completely lost in this bloody desert with 16 tanks and God knows how many trucks and vehicles behind me waiting to get to RHQ. Here we were about to go into action for the first time and I had made a complete and utter cock-up and I could have cheerfully murdered Charles and shot myself on the spot when, suddenly, out of the blue a staff car appeared and who should get out but our Brigadier, 'Boomer' Watkins. He recognised me and in his deep, sepulchral voice he said, "Hello Hamilton, it's you. I suppose you are looking for the 8th Tanks?" "Yes sir, I am." "Well, I think you will find them about a mile over there as I have just come from them. Good luck, off you go." This time I took a very careful compass bearing and I could see the stars by then and I made my driver reel off pretty well every tenth of a mile and suddenly I had to yell out "Halt" as we nearly crashed into about half-a-dozen people grouped round three or four cars. Thank God! we had reached RHQ at last.

The Adjutant, Brian McCabe, later to command 'A' Squadron and who got severely wounded at Alamein where he was awarded a Bar to his MC, came rushing up saying, "Where the bloody hell have you been! Can't you read a bloody compass or a map, etc." Fortunately dear old George had come along at that time and said to Brian that we had been told there would be a hurricane lamp on the top of a staff car for guiding us in and he said "The blasted lamp is down on the ground and with all these vehicles around we couldn't see it so it was not Ham's fault."

From that moment onwards I was George's devoted slave for life and particularly as we walked away he put his arm around my shoulders and grinned and said, "Well done Ham! you got us here eventually: no need to worry: it happens to everyone all the time!"

We crossed through The Wire, I would think, somewhere between two and three o'clock in the morning to the accompaniment of a really tremendous thunderstorm with flashes of lightning and in my febrile imagination I wondered whether it was a hell of a battle but of course it wasn't - it was just a thunderstorm.

'B' Squadron was then attached to the 5th New Zealand Brigade and on the 21st November we were told that we were going to do a dawn attack with the 23rd New Zealand Battalion on Fort Capuzzo. This was a small fort consisting of low white buildings with a low white stone wall around it with one or two turrets, rather like a fort from Beau Geste. It was right on the frontier and because we had crossed The Wire we were attacking from behind them. In other words we were attacking from the west to take them in the rear.

We attacked with three Troops up and George and two Troops in reserve and I was on the extreme right with the Maori Infantry in bren gun carriers coming up behind us.

I was then suddenly aware of unpleasant things screaming and whistling past the side of the turret and over my head and in complete and utter naive astonishment I turned round to my gunner and exclaimed, "Good God! they're shooting at us!" His reply was much more lurid and we immediately opened fire ourselves in the classic Lulworth Gunnery School style of having the tank broadside on to the target and on the move - the idea being that it was more difficult for a stationary gun to hit a moving target. However, although the Valentine 2-pdr had a powered all round traverse the elevation and the depression was done by a shoulder mounting - yes! a ruddy shoulder mounting! The gun therefore was bouncing up and down and in exasperation I ordered my driver to swing right and to halt, so that we were then head-on to the target. We rapidly loosed off a few rounds of

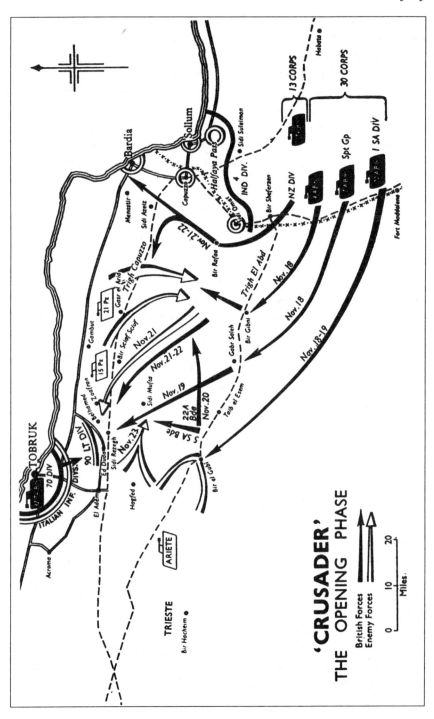

'CRUSADER'
THE OPENING PHASE

British Forces
Enemy Forces

0   10   20
Miles.

13 CORPS

30 CORPS

4 IND. DIV.

NZ DIV

R.A.F.

Spt Gp

A.A.Bde.

1 SA DIV

S.A.R.

Nov. 18

Nov. 18

Nov. 18-19

Habata

Sidi Suleiman

Bir Sheferzen

Fort Maddalena

Sollum

Halfaya Pass

Capuzzo

Sidi Omar

Bardia

Menastir

Sidi Azeiz

Bir Rafsa

Trigh el Abd

Trigh Capuzzo

Nov. 21-22

21 Pz

Gasr el Arid

Gambut

15 Pz

Bir Sciaf Sciuf

Nov. 21

Nov. 21-22

Bel Hamed

Zaafran

Sidi Mufta

Nov. 19

Gabr Saleh

Bir Gubni

Nov. 20

Tarb el Esem

22 A Bde

5 SA Bde

Nov. 23

Sidi Rezegh

Ed Duda

El Adem

Hagfed

Bir el Gubi

TOBRUK

70 DIV

90 LT DIV

ITALIAN INF. DIVS.

Acroma

ARIETE

TRIESTE

Bir Hacheim

2-pdr and then smartened up the place with Besa machine-gun fire.

There was a certain amount of shell fire coming at us, not very heavy, but as this was our first experience of coming under enemy fire it seemed quite heavy at that time. I then noticed some guns way out to my right so I ordered the Troop to swing right and go for them. If only I had had the sense to look at the map that I had with me I would have then noticed that they were marked U/S - which meant that they were not in use being unserviceable - and when in fact we got up to them we found they were abandoned.

However, we were then overlooking Hellfire Pass down into Sollum Bay and I could see vehicles rapidly descending the pass so we opened up with both 2-pdr and Besa fire, knocking out two or three and saw troops scurrying from them. We tried shooting up the barracks and buildings as well but then I thought that we had better return to Fort Capuzzo as I could hear quite a bit of fire coming from there.

I then ordered the Troop to rally on me and return to Capuzzo Barracks at once. All my training had stressed that tanks did not go into and amongst buildings on their own as they could so easily get knocked out by Molotov Cocktails (petrol bombs) because we were so blind. I therefore halted my Troop about 300 yards away from the fort and started to walk in on foot, but as there was a certain amount of stuff flying around and I couldn't see any tanks outside the fort, I thought that this was damn silly so I ran back to my tank and into the fort we went.

We came across a couple of lorries in stone sangars and shot them up and also, to my gunner's delight, a nice eight-wheeled German armoured car which we similarly shot-up and then we concentrated on plastering the buildings with both 2-pdr and Besa. The wireless then suddenly started crackling again and George ordered us to pull back and rendezvous outside.

When I went and reported to him he looked at me rather sternly and wanted to know just where the hell I'd been and why hadn't I gone into the fort with the rest of the Squadron? I explained that I had seen the guns and gone off to attack them but then found they were U/S so had shot-up some transport going down Hellfire Pass to Sollum, also two trucks and an armoured car inside the fort. He then relaxed a little and told me in future not to go swanning off on my own because the essential thing was for the Squadron to keep together for maximum effort and support. I was certainly learning very fast indeed.

The next day we mopped up around Sollum itself and the two operations netted about 300 to 400 prisoners, several transports knocked out (including my armoured car) and several guns so we were feeling pretty pleased with ourselves in this our first action.

Early that morning I observed an Italian lorry coming down the dusty track towards our position and, with my binoculars, I could see the two Itie soldiers laughing and talking happily with each other and obviously quite unaware that Capuzzo had been captured by us and I smiled visualising what would happen when they suddenly realised that they were to go in the bag. However, I was the one to be surprised because George, almost at the same time, came up on the air and ordered me to shoot them up. I mildly protested, saying that it was not necessary as we were about to put them in the bag, but he immediately came back on the air again and angrily ordered me to open fire. I procrastinated a bit more and then reported, rather smugly, that we had in fact captured them and their lorry. A little later he drew me to one side and sternly told me the next time he gave me an order I was to damn well act on it and if it was an order to open fire then I was to act bloody quickly indeed. He walked away and left me feeling rather upset and it was not until some weeks later, when he was talking to me, that he said that he was seriously concerned with me and my attitude at Capuzzo and he seriously thought that he would have to replace me as a Troop Leader because he didn't think that I had enough aggression and that I was far too soft. Then he laughed and clapped me hard on the back saying, "But Ham! that all changed after Sidi Rezegh because there you were blooded and there you grew up!"

Sidi Rezegh

That night we were just about to start our evening meal when a real flap order came through. We were to drop everything, start up, mount and to proceed immediately along the Trigh Capuzzo track as fast as we possibly could. We were then to link up with the rest of the Brigade and other armour and infantry who were then engaged in desperate fighting at Sidi Rezegh.

The main battle area was some 15-20 miles south-east of Tobruk and a big armoured battle was raging there. It was going to be a pretty hairy move for us as we had never ever done a forced night march like this before - and it was over completely unknown territory. We set off, as far as I can remember, at about seven o'clock in the evening and as

'A' Squadron was with us there were about 30 tanks or so together with the 'A' Echelon lorries and so on. The distance was a good 70 miles or more, which meant some five or six hours motoring at the speed we could move at, and within a few minutes we were covered in clouds of choking, blinding dust and sand. After about five hours of this one was absolutely exhausted and I was petrified when suddenly three or four black objects appeared in front of me and before I could give my driver the order to halt we crashed through some tents. I jumped out, terrified that we would find some bodies in them but Thank God! they were empty. I hate to think what the owners said when they came back and found out what had happened to them.

Shortly after this we reached our rendezvous area, which speaks volumes for the splendid navigation, and also the expertise of the drivers, over such a long distance under these conditions at night. It was now about one o'clock in the morning and we had to refuel of course before bedding down for the night in our leaguer position. This consisted of the tanks on the outer ring with all the soft transport being inside and in any group of three tanks one had to be on sentry duty and wireless watch. As we had to stand to an hour before dawn this meant we only had about three or four hours sleep and this was the standard procedure from then onwards.

As soon as it was daybreak we fanned out in battle formation and immediately started getting down to breakfast when, once again, a flap message came through that there was a strong enemy armoured column approaching us four to five miles to the south and we, that is 'B' Squadron, were to proceed immediately down the wadi in front of us and up to the escarpment at the top to engage and hold. My Troop, number 9, was the lead Troop for the day so we shot off flat out down to the bottom of the wadi, went on for about 300 yards or so, then slowed right down to disperse any dust clouds and I gave the signal to my Troop to turn left, form line and very slowly start to climb up to the top of the escarpment.

My Sergeant was on my left and my Corporal on my right and in order to get a perfect turret-down position I was actually standing on my Tank Commander's seat so that the top of the turret was half-way up my thighs and I had my binoculars in one hand and the microphone to my driver in the other.

As we were coming to the top of the crest at about four or five mph there was suddenly the most tremendous crash on the left side of the

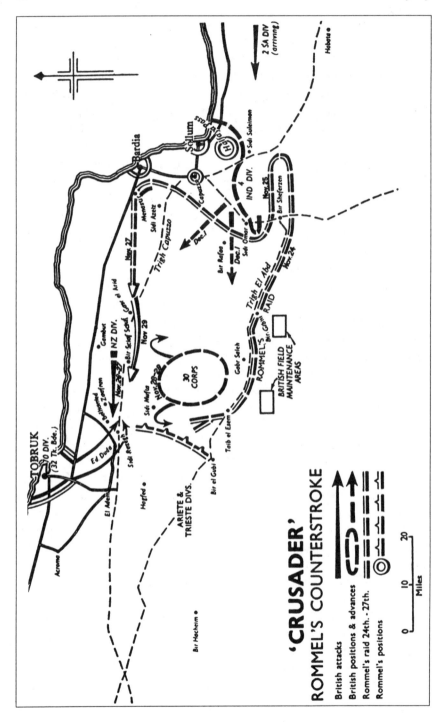

'CRUSADER'

ROMMEL'S COUNTERSTROKE

British attacks

British positions & advances

Rommel's raid 24th.- 27th.

Rommel's positions

0   10   20

Miles

turret, a sheet of flame flickered round my legs and I was temporarily concussed by the blast and blinded by something which splashed all over my eyes and face. When I shook my head clear and wiped my face with my hands, which came away all bloody and messy, I looked down into the smoking interior of the turret and saw that the wireless immediately alongside me was well and truly on fire, there were two smoke-blackened holes in the left side of the turret and my gunner was slumped over the gun minus most of the left side of his face and the top of his head, and I was splattered with his blood and brains.

Out of the corner of my eye to my left I could see that Troop Sergeant Tilford's tank appeared to be on fire because the idiot had forgotten to jettison some spare cans of diesel he had been carrying on the outside and they had been hit and set alight.

However Corporal Callister was banging away merrily and the rest of the Squadron was coming up rapidly on my left and deploying.

I yelled to my driver to go down back to the bottom of the wadi so that we could put the fire out and to see what I could do for my poor gunner because, incredibly, he still seemed to be alive but breathing shuddering, gasping breaths. We pulled him out and I gingerly tried to put a first-aid dressing on the awful wound on his head, but it was quite useless as he died whilst I did that.

There was a hell of a racket going on all around me, not only from the Squadron, which was heavily engaged on the top of the escarpment, but, inadvertently, we had stopped about 15-20 yards smack in front of a New Zealand 25-pdr Battery and they were blasting forth with rapid fire right over the top of our heads.

Suddenly, with all this hellish noise, I heard the whining scream of engines and looked up to see about 20 Stuka dive-bombers coming down for us with nasty looking black blobs in front of them and as I hurled myself flat on the deck I was lifted up and slammed down again by the blast of the exploding bombs.

Now all that happened just about as quickly as you are taking time to read this and I remember very clearly indeed that when I looked down into the smoking interior of my turret, after we were hit, and saw what had happened to my poor gunner, saying grimly to myself, "Christ Almighty! Stu! - this is war" and in that moment I grew up from the naive, innocent young idiot I had been the day or so before.

*   *   *

The Squadron acquitted itself well, seeing off the opposition eventually and inflicting quite heavy losses and fortunately receiving comparatively light casualties itself. I moved back to our old leaguer area and stopped en route at a Field Dressing Station so that the medical orderlies could take care of poor young Cormack's body. Whilst there I met one of our Squadron Sergeants who had been lightly wounded in the leg and helped him into the tent, but fortunately his wound was very light. It was an enormous marquee and it was crammed with wounded, from light to very serious indeed. There must have been about 300 or so in the tent and it was a horrible sight. I was impressed with the extraordinary courageous, stoical calm most of the men seemed to be showing as there was very little noise, but the smell and the sights really were quite horrible.

I was very pleased indeed to get outside and to breath in some deep lungfuls of clean fresh air and thank God I wasn't in there myself and I prayed hard that I never would be.

When I got into the leaguer area I immediately reported to George, who came to have a look at my tank and he looked at me rather curiously and asked if I was OK. I was rather surprised at his remark and said of course I was. He asked me then if I had been hit myself and again I was surprised and said "no" and then I suddenly realised that I probably looked a bit shocked and my overalls looked very messy, indeed stained, and I probably had blood on my face as well.

We immediately set to refuelling and re-ammoing and regrouping the tanks and the Squadron fitters came up to take out the burnt-out wireless set and fit in a new one whilst I got some petrol from them and swabbed and cleaned out the inside of the turret. At the same time I ordered my driver to get a meal going because we had had no breakfast and it was somewhere after midday by now. He looked horrified at this and I irritably told him to do it straight away because heaven knows when we would get another chance for a meal. I think really he was in a state of shock himself and couldn't believe that anybody would want to eat under those circumstances and he and a few others who heard me probably thought I was a bit callous and hard-hearted about it, but this was war and, damn it, life had to go on.

The penetration had happened by the opening on the turret to sling out empty shell cases, just above the gunner's head, and I suggested that the fitters welded-up such openings on all the remaining tanks in the Squadron as I felt sure that this was a contribution to Cormack's death.

It was just as well that I got Tpr. Bainbridge to prepare a meal because no sooner had we finished when an order came through that we were to carry out a sweep over the top of the escarpment where we had had the scrap in the morning. George wanted another Troop to be the lead Troop but I vigorously protested saying that I wanted to carry on with it for the rest of the day as it was my job. Accordingly we went out once again and swept about 12 or more miles further south. It was getting dark by then and as we had seen nothing of the enemy we were just about to turn back and return to our leaguer when I suddenly spotted, in the dim distance, a large group of people and vehicles. I reported on the air to George who told me to investigate but to go forward carefully and find out who and what they were.

So we shot off and the closer we came to them the more puzzled I was because the vehicles were all stationary, wrecked, burnt, derelict and the whole area was littered with the debris of war as far as I could see: wrecked vehicles, overturned guns, abandoned equipment and stores. I then noticed some further movement over to my right, figures moving about, and a fairly large crowd of people, many lying on the ground, but whether they were ours or the enemy I couldn't make out.

We slowly advanced nearer to them and three men came forward with their hands up. I jumped down from my tank with my revolver out and found out that the leading man was a British Medical Officer with two South African orderlies. I gave them some cigarettes and told my gunner to radio George informing him what was happening and the MO then told me what had happened. Apparently a day-and-a-half earlier an entire South African Infantry Brigade and its transport had been caught by a large German tank force and practically annihilated.

What he and these orderlies had been doing was going round and collecting the wounded into a group and getting walking wounded to go round to the vehicles to pick up any rations or equipment, blankets and in particular get hold of any water, draining radiators if necessary, because nobody knew when they were going to be picked up. The night before a German armoured car patrol had come up to them and the armoured car commander was a fine bloke and gave them what help he could, offering them medical supplies from the meagre equipment on the armoured cars, also cigarettes etc. and told them in broken English that they would be OK because they were going to be put in the bag the next day as the Germans had had a big victory that day and pretty well defeated us.

The next morning, which was the morning we had this scrap, when the column came back, being a mixed column of German and Italian troops, the Italians behaved in a completely different manner. They roughly searched the men, pinched cigarette cases, wrist watches, wallets, anything from them, jeered at them and even sited their anti-tank guns in and behind the wounded so that if we followed up from the morning battle we couldn't open fire because of the wounded lying down in front. Bastards.

We radioed back to our area and arranged for a fleet of ambulances to come out and pick up the more seriously wounded and we ourselves picked up as many walking wounded or slightly wounded men as we could and piled them up onto the back of the tanks, and turned round and went back to our own leaguer area. In actual fact we saved something like 134 men that evening so I felt that young Cormack's death had been somewhat avenged. He was the first to be killed in the Squadron.

The next day, November 27th was pretty hectic. Constant shelling, aerial bombing, alarms and flaps: going out to see off unidentified vehicles: the odd scrap or two and/or going to the assistance of infantry calling for our help. This carried right on through until the afternoon of the next day, the 28th, and we had just moved back into our leaguer area to refuel and re-ammo when an order came through that we were to advance immediately to break up a threatened German counter-attack.

The sun was setting in an angry blood-orange scene in the west and George could only muster about eight or nine of us, out of 16, and in we went, bald-headed, without any support of any description: we just had to go in as far and as fast as possible and break it up.

I think the very speed and audacity of our attack took the Germans completely by surprise because in spite of them flinging absolutely everything at us, 88's, 75's, 50mm, mortars, machine-gun fire, the whole lot, we actually overran their positions and got right in amongst them so that the German infantry were jumping out of their slit trenches and running in all directions. My tank had been hit several times by then and one anti-tank shell had practically jammed the turret ring so that we could hardly traverse the gun at all. The only way I could engage a target was to swing the whole tank about which was not conducive to rapid and accurate fire.

It was almost completely dark by now and I had stopped and my gunner was engaging some target when I was suddenly aware of a burst of machine-gun fire from immediately behind me and extremely close too and in the darkness I could see the tracer and bullets flicking off the turret all around me. When I turned around in alarm and consternation to see where the hell it was coming from I noticed, in the gloom, about 20 yards away a tank with its commander waving at me. I couldn't think what the hell he was waving for because it was no party as far as I was concerned, as I was shit scared.

I found out afterwards that it was Sgt. Simpkins who had been following me and seen me overrun some enemy slit-trenches and then stop to engage a target. About eight to ten German soldiers then got out and started to run away in all directions except for one very brave soldier who was actually clambering up the back of my tank, over the engine covers, with a stick grenade in his hand to chuck into the open turret. Simpkins realised that there was no possible chance of warning me so he ordered his gunner to open fire with his Besa and shoot him off. He said that he was a bit concerned that I was in the line of fire and my God! I certainly was! He gave me the fright of my life but he certainly saved my life that day and few weeks later he went on to win a very good Military Medal.

It was completely dark by now and we seemed to have achieved our objective in that we had broken up the counter-attack and the enemy appeared to have melted away. I could only see two other tanks nearby, nothing was happening on the wireless, which seemed quite dead, the enemy fire had slackened right off and as my turret was almost jammed I decided the only thing to do was to collect what tanks I could and pull back.

We obviously couldn't stay up on the objective on our own, without any infantry support at all, and anyway we were very short on fuel and ammunition by then. So I did this and the remaining two tanks followed me back to our leaguer, which was quite difficult to find in the pitch dark.

The reason there was nothing happening on the wireless and why I couldn't see any other tanks was that the six of them had all been hit and disabled. George did a magnificent job here going round in the dark - so close to the enemy that he could hear the Jerries talking to one another - collecting the crews, including some pretty badly wounded: encouraging them and giving them cigarettes to help boost their morale, helping with first-aid, etc. Eventually he got hold of some

German wooden ammunition trollies to put the wounded men on and then got them back to our lines. This is where he won his DSO.

The next afternoon, after a pretty hectic morning, we were wearily taking a breather but keeping a wary eye open as there was a certain amount of shelling going on and there appeared to be quite a bit of movement according to dust clouds on the near horizon, the wireless suddenly crackled in my head-phones.

Dear old George often didn't bother to use correct wireless code names and he came up on the air and said, "Hello Ham - have you any nivea? Over."

I quickly looked at my codes which were written in chinagraph on my map case - couldn't find the word "nivea" - so asked for a repeat message.

Rather irritatedly he repeated his request and again I replied that I didn't understand and would he please "say again."

A real blast this time, "Wake up you dozy sod! Have you any Nivea cream? My face is bloody sore..."

Hardly the sort of message to expect under these circumstances and what we would say was "A typical George!" No wonder the men thought so highly of him.

The next day, the 29th, was pretty similar with constant shelling, bombing, and flaps with a group of about five or six of us, which was all we could muster, trying to fend off probing attacks of enemy tanks and trying to hold the position for our own very battered and weary infantry. Late that afternoon when it was just getting dark and I was the last tank to come in I noticed a lone figure, running and waving to me, about 300 yards away so I turned the tank around and went back to pick him up.

He was a very exhausted New Zealand infantryman. He lent against the tank and let forth a stream of invective saying he was "fucking well fed-up with the fucking war and the fucking desert and he was fucked if he was going to do any fucking more."

I told him that if he would only get on the back then we could "fucking move off." He did, and I had the gun reversed over the tail to fend off anything coming after us and he was standing over the driver's hatch with his back to the way we were going. Just as we were approaching our leaguer area in the dark - everyone being very trigger happy - to my horror a Bofors gun opened up at us at ground level firing a clip of five 40mm shells at about 60 yards range. It was incredible seeing the red tracer screaming and whipping past the sides and turret but, fortunately, the shooting was appallingly bad and Thank God! They never hit us.

However, the Kiwi soldier frantically jumped off and went running away into the dark saying, "he was fucking well going to fuck off for ever as he was fucked if he was going to hang about and fucking well get shot up by his own fucking troops!"

During this time, when we were in the region of Point 175, we had pulled back into leaguer to refuel and re-ammo, and it was almost dark after a very heavy day.

I was in the turret helping to stow away the ammo and I just looked out of the top towards a ridge about 600 yards away and, to my astonishment, I saw a Panzer Mark III lumber over the top, turn sideways and stop. I immediately jumped into the gunner's seat, yelled to him to come and help me load, and opened fire. My first shot was just short but my second was a direct hit. I slammed in three more for good measure and the turret flaps opened and out jumped the crew.

I then switched to Besa machine-gun fire and fired as they tried to get back over the crest and two of them dropped and remained still. This may seem very callous now but at that time it was different entirely. Our crews were being shot at when they bailed out so it seemed entirely and perfectly justifiable to me to do the same to the Jerry crews.

On a completely different tack - I have been asked, since the end of the war, that as I suffer from claustrophobia, how on earth did I get on inside a tank? The simple answer to that is that in 'B' Squadron, at least, I didn't; we never fought with the turret lids closed down.

The turret flaps on the Valentine opened flat - fore and aft - through 180 degrees so that from a distance it looked as if the flaps were closed. If closed down then one was completely blind just looking through a three inch thick glass visor in one direction only. It was so much quicker and therefore safer to stick one's head out - have a quick 'shufti' all around - and then duck down inside again.

Again, whilst in Italy, with the Sherman tank I never fought closed down for the above reason. Anyway, the fumes and noise from the 75mm gun almost made this impossible. The Sherman flaps however only opened sideways, at about a 45 degree angle, which was of course a dead giveaway.

Still I survived, even though I very nearly bought it at Sidi Rezegh in

1941 - "Thank you Sgt. Simpkins!"

The Regiment had taken one hell of a bashing by then and we were ordered to go into Tobruk and hand over what tanks we had left to the 4th RTR. We could only muster seven out of 52 and of these at least three or four, like mine were badly damaged.

George's World War One wisdom and experience came into force here because one of the tank drivers, who was a pretty tough cookie, was acting in a very strange manner being withdrawn and very depressed and we guessed it was some form of shellshock. So George got hold of his Troop Leader and told him that, by hook or crook, he was to get hold of some hot water and a complete change of clothing for this man. He was to get him to have a complete wash and shave and then to put on a clean shirt, trousers and overalls. This was done and the driver's depression and withdrawal symptoms disappeared on the spot. He had been so shattered with the recent events and so utterly depressed with everything but this wash and change of clothes worked a miracle.

Another thing which George did was not so popular but again it worked. As we were doing comparatively little after handing over our tanks he decided that it would be a good idea to smarten everybody up by having a Squadron parade, what remained of the Squadron that is, and to do some drill and marching and saluting. This naturally gave several disgruntled people the opportunity to let off steam and grumble about 'bloody bullshit! What the hell!' etc., but it certainly took one's mind off what we had experienced going through these last few hectic and grim weeks.

My driver, L/Cpl. Field, had been slightly wounded in the leg so I had been given a replacement who was unfortunately pretty useless. He came up to me one evening and rather excitedly exclaimed "Sir! I've got hold of a sack of Itie flour so we can have some bully-beef fritters this evening." "Good, that will make a change" I said. When I came back later from SHQ there was the most awful smell and un-appetizing mess in the frying pan because it wasn't flour that he had got hold of - it was size. He went into Tobruk with our few remaining tanks and, unfortunately for him, he was put in the bag when the Jerries recaptured it. I cannot say, in all honesty, that I was particularly sorry to lose him.

Somewhere about the night of December 2/3rd the 8th RTR were told that we were being pulled out and that we were to be transported right back to The Wire for a refit and rest. We set off in 3-ton lorries and mine was being driven by a wild-eyed Maori who seemed to have but two positions for the throttle and brake. Either the throttle was flat down on the floor or it was the brake on the floor, much to the shouts and yells of disgust from the wretched men in the back who were being banged about all over the place.

It was quite a hairy move to start with because the situation was extremely fluid with groups of Germans, Italians and ourselves scattered around just everywhere and nobody knew who was who, particularly at night. Everyone was also extremely jittery after the last few weeks of very hectic fighting and activity so that sentries were very trigger-happy, to say the least, opening fire first before asking for some out-dated password or who we were.

We actually had a burst of Bren-gun fire right through the top of our lorry, thank God, because it didn't hurt anyone, but the language and the obscenities from inside were quite unprintable. We eventually got back intact down near The Wire at Bir Enba and thankfully and happily got down to some blessed sleep.

We were then hastily re-equipped with fresh Valentines - when I say fresh - these were tanks which had been recovered from the battlefield and then put back into, allegedly, battle-fit condition and handed over to us for further operations.

We immediately set to and got them properly fit to our kind of specification, i.e. we removed all the ammunition bin liners as these would only hold about 60 rounds of 2-pdr which was nothing like enough: instead we got hold of old tin water containers, cut them in half and then stacked them all round the turret and this way we could pack in about 100 rounds of 2-pdr or more. We did the same with the Besa machine-gun ammo so we were literally a travelling ammunition dump.

Whilst in this area I came in late one evening from a patrol or an exercise and just managed to get a meal in the Regimental Mess Tent. There was only one other officer there, Peter Gray from HQ Squadron and we both had a beer, then a whisky, and as I was very tired we walked out to our tents.

It was a pitch black night with not a light to be seen and after walking about 200-300 yards or so I said, "Hey Peter! we've overshot the tent lines" so we turned and retraced our steps. Damned if we could find them! So we split up, about 10 yards apart, and started to quarter the area.

After some time we realised that we were hopelessly lost - the moon had come up by then - and we saw something shining away in the distance. It was a pile of discarded petrol cans so we made a rough shelter out of them and lay down on the cold, bare sand.

As we were wearing only shirts and shorts it was bitterly cold and sleep was very fitful. By dawn I was awake and could just see that we were in a shallow depression, so I walked to its rim and could see vehicles on either horizon. We tossed a coin and walked towards one group who turned out to be a crowd of RASC and they said that the 8th RTR were on the other horizon!

When we eventually got back we were greeted with hoots of derision as Peter was the Regimental Recce Officer and I was the Squadron Recce Officer.

Peter had a very lucky escape after Bardia had been captured. He was swanning around outside the area with Sgt. Major Alexander, looking for loot he said (!), and they were captured by an Italian patrol. S/M Alexander was put in their truck and an Italian lieutenant went with Peter in his Dodge truck.

For some unknown reason Peter had taken his revolver belt off and had left it lying on the seat of the Dodge, under a pullover, in between himself and the Itie lieutenant.

He asked the Itie if he would like a cigarette? A good one? Players? The Itie replied "Si! si! Buono!" So Peter put his hand under the pullover, pulled the trigger and shot him in the side. He then opened the door, pushed him out and drove off like the clappers.

When the Italian soldiers realised what had happened they vented their fury on the luckless S/M Alexander and roughed him up with fists, boots and rifle butts. However he managed to escape a day or so later and got back to us, none the worse except for quite a few bruises.

There was no question of a rest as we had to knock new crews into shape as quickly as possible, as we were then attached to the lst South African Division to do the attack on the port and town of Bardia. This was the only place of importance left in Axis hands in Cyrenaica because both the Germans and Italians had pulled right back from Tobruk and retreated towards the Tripolitanian border down at El Agheila.

Bardia

In those days Bardia was considered to be strongly held with a mixed force of German and Italian troops totalling 10,000 to 12,000 men and there was a perimeter wire stretching some 13 to 14 miles all round it. This perimeter defence consisted of, firstly, a triple roll of barbed-wire about ten feet high and eight feet in width, behind which was a wide and steep concrete anti-tank ditch and a wide minefield behind the ditch. There was then a second row of triple barbed wire and a further minefield and a third row of triple barbed wire and behind that of course were the main FDL's (forward defensive lines), that is dug-in anti-tank guns, machine-gun posts, infantry slit trenches, and so on, with the main artillery further back still.

The attack was to go in just before dawn on the morning of December 31st and it was to be all round the perimeter. The 8th Tanks had the job of attacking on the right flank and 'B' Squadron was on the extreme right of the attack.

We were more or less in our battle positions, a few miles behind the start line, and orders were given that there was to be no noise or movement of any kind with everything camouflaged, when one morning I was rather surprised to see a truck come roaring up to me creating a huge cloud of dust. It stopped alongside my tank and out stepped a chap wearing the most extraordinary headgear I had ever seen and he turned out to be a Polish captain of artillery, the first Pole I had met.

He spoke quite good English and asked me to explain the situation and point out enemy positions on the map because his 25-pdr Battery was going to give us some support. I got my map out and started to point out the Italian positions and then the German ones and he stopped me and said, "Where are the Germans?" I pointed them out again saying , "they're here and here and here."

He then immediately turned round and spoke rapidly and, of course incomprehensibly, in Polish to a sergeant in the truck who grinned widely and got onto a wireless set. I asked the officer what was going on and he looked at me, smiled, and said, "just wait a moment." I did and, suddenly, about three minutes later there was a most tremendous crash as eight 25-pdrs opened up rapid fire on the German positions. I was absolutely horrified and told him to stop immediately because under no circumstances were we allowed to give away our positions. Whilst we were arguing furiously about this and the guns were still blasting away George came roaring up and wanted to know just what the hell was going on.

It transpired that this Pole was one of many unfortunates who were captured by the Russians when they moved into Poland, in collaboration with the Germans, and had been sent to a prisoner of war camp in Siberia with hundreds of others. Eventually General Anders managed to get a whole Corps out from there and they had travelled down through Palestine to the Western Desert. This was his first chance to have a crack back at the Nazis since 1939 and he simply couldn't wait.

This was my first experience of meeting Polish troops, though I was to get to know them pretty well in Italy towards the end of the war in 1945. I don't think, however, that this little episode of the gunner opening fire when he should not have done so made the slightest difference to anything, though it must have satisfied his sense of pride.

As the attack on Bardia was imminent, being scheduled for dawn on December 31st, Christmas was quietly celebrated in our Forward Assembly Area.

On Christmas Eve I was in the little tent that 'B' Squadron was using as a mess, decorating the oilskin table-cloth with chinagraph pencils, when I heard the sound of soft voices and the shuffling of feet nearby so I went outside to see what was going on.

It was a wonderfully clear night with the heavens absolutely ablaze with myriads of stars which seemed to be so low that one felt it was possible to touch them - and it was utterly quiet and still. Our Padre, Sam Kemble, had collected about half-a-dozen or more men to form a choir and they were visiting each Squadron to sing Christmas hymns and carols. There were also some 20-30 'B' Squadron tank crew men assembled with them.

The quiet singing of these hymns and carols in this superb setting was marvellous and very moving and brought a lump to one's throat. Then one of the choir named Joe Brogan, who I believe was Welsh, stepped forward and with his fine baritone voice he sang, so poignantly, "Silent Night," whilst the others just hummed the melody. I will never, ever forget the way his powerful voice rang out through the still, silent desert night... it was sheer magic. It brought the thought of my lovely wife so close to me that, as young and as hardbitten as I was then, I just had to walk away into the dark, silent desert on my own.

Even now, some 50 years later, I can still capture that magic when I hear that hymn sung.

The attack was due to start at about 4.30am on the morning of December 31st so by about 3am we moved up very slowly and very quietly indeed to our start line. The drill was that the South African Engineers would cut the wire of the first fence and set off Bangalore Torpedoes to blow up the anti-tank ditch, fill it in, lift the mines and then cut the wire on the second fence and mark the gaps on both so we could go through.

We waited nervously and tensely in complete silence in the dark until there was the explosion of the Bangalore Torpedoes going off and about 25 minutes later George came up on the air saying, "Hello George 9 - off you go - out." My Troop was to lead the attack so naturally I was the first tank to go through. We charged through the gap in the first wire, bumped over the filled-in anti-tank ditch, again through the second gap and past through the third lot of wire and then, as we had rehearsed, my driver had strict instructions to measure off a three-quarters of a mile on his speedometer before turning right to take the enemy in the rear.

My gunner was firing short, sharp bursts of Besa machine-gun fire three to four hundred yards ahead to keep the enemy heads down and as we swung right to take them in the rear I was being clouted all over the left side of the turret with gun flashes everywhere and my driver was yelling out, "anti-tank guns half left 100 yards."

There was another devastating crash on the left side of the turret and, once again, I was temporarily concussed and blinded by stuff flying around inside but when I opened my eyes this time, thank God! it was to see my young gunner, Nobby Clarke, staring up in absolute astonishment because immediately over the top of his head was the glowing, red-hot nose of an anti-tank shell which had penetrated the armour and then stuck with the solid nose cone about two inches inside.

As I have already said, it was just above his head and slap in line with my heart because I was standing, as usual, with my head out of the top of the turret.

My driver, a good man, L/Cpl. Field, had automatically swung the tank hard left to charge the anti-tank gun and before it fired again we literally smashed into it, and the crew, machine-gunning them as we did so.

What I didn't realise was that the maps we had been given with enemy positions were faulty and the enemy were much further back from the third wire obstacle than a half mile so that when I turned right, hoping to take them in the rear, I had actually turned and was going broadside right across their defences. Another thing I wasn't aware of at the time was that the reason we were attracting all the gun fire was that Corporal Clee's tank, on coming up to the entrance of the anti-tank ditch, had stalled the engine because there had suddenly been a complete electrical fault and the driver couldn't get it started. Sergeant Tilford, my Troop Sergeant, literally had to push him out of the way before the rest of the Squadron could get through so this meant that old Joe Soap was the only tank through for about five minutes and attracted rather a lot of unnecessary attention.

The attack was completely successful and we penetrated, I should think, something like ten miles inside until we came to the very steep impassable wadis and we could look down from the top of the escarpment onto the town and harbour of Bardia itself and all sorts of panic stations were going on down there. It was rather marvellous.

We had comparatively light casualties as we swung around mopping up, taking prisoners all over the place, though unfortunately a couple of 88s had knocked out a few tanks until one of them which unfortunately had killed his best friend Tony Read a little earlier was summarily dealt with by Hicky Sugden (Major, MC and Bar).

The attack had been more successful in the centre so we were told to stay in our positions until dark and then to pull back to our rendezvous area. As we had been up since 3am that morning and it was now somewhere about 7 or 8pm and we had had a pretty busy time in between, no one was more pleased than myself to get the order from George to pull out and get back to base.

I ordered my driver to swing left about and as he did there was the most tremendous Bang! and a flash and the tank seemed to jump about a foot in the air and lurched to a stop as we ran over an anti-tank mine which smashed the tracks and suspension.

So we had to spend New Year's Eve cold, tired, hungry, wet - as it started to drizzle - and frightened at being in a broken-down tank in an enemy minefield some six miles behind enemy lines and I cursed bitterly at the thought of all the 'Gabardine Swine' jazzing it up in Cairo and Alex with all the lovely popsies. Some people have all the luck.

We couldn't stay in the turret all night because if any enemy patrols came up to us we would need to have the engine running to operate the power-traverse and this would be a dead giveaway. So the driver and my gunner lay underneath the front end of the tank with their revolvers and the dismounted Besa machine-gun whilst I was at the rear with my revolver and a tommy-gun as I thought this would be the best means of defence against any marauding patrols. Although there were all sorts of noises, bangs and unpleasantness going on all around us for most of the night with Very lights, flares, etc. nobody thank God! attacked us. We were very pleased indeed when dawn came up and the fitters eventually came to our rescue enabling us to get back to the Squadron feeling very tired and bedraggled. Without doubt that was the most wretched, miserable and lousy New Year's Eve in my life.

Around about January 4th our CO had a conference and he told us that we were going to be lifted on tank transporters back up west again, right up to Benghazi and beyond and that we were to get ready for this.

According to my diary we moved on January 8th on these transporters past Tobruk and Mechili and reached Msus, which was south and past Benghazi, on January 13th. We were then approximately 1000 miles from rear base at Alexandria and some 650 miles from railhead at Mersa Matruh so we were well and truly 'up in the blue.'

The RASC lieutenant who was in charge of the transporters, was a pretty awful type with sleek dark hair and a thin Errol Flynn pencil moustache, but as he was on his own we took pity on him and we asked him if he would like to join us for the evening meal.

The Mess consisted, as usual, of a 3-ton lorry-top on the deck with a small table and few chairs and, as he was an RASC man, we naturally thought that he would bring along a bottle or a few extra rations.

Not a bit of it. He drank most of our meagre ration of beer and whisky, tucked into our rations and then cleaned us out at poker. This last item particularly irked Reggie and Douglas who thought that they were pretty good at cards. I am glad to say we never saw him again.

We were now attached to the 4th Indian Division - another very fine 8th Army formation - and were part of an exceptionally thin line right up at the sharp end.

The 8th Army was stretched to its absolute limit of its long line of communications and as it had taken some pretty heavy casualties in the preceding battles in November and December 1941, units were being pulled back for very necessary regrouping, reforming and re-equipping.

Also, though we did not know this at the time, the 8th Army was being denuded of supplies and reinforcements which were diverted, tragically, to Singapore.

When Rommel started to come out, cautiously, with probing tanks and armoured cars, more or less on reconnaissance, panic buttons were hit left, right and centre back at Rear Army Headquarters and units were told to pull back as fast as possible. This was because there was no point in hanging on to a few hundred square miles of featureless desert at the expense of more men and armour which were desperately needed. The ensuing commotion then was chronic.

The flap really started around January 22nd and 23rd; my diary has brief notes that on the 23rd we covered something like 88 miles at night moving back from Msus to east of Benghazi. The flap continued and on the 25th we covered a further 74 miles back to the area around Barce.

We had pulled off the road to leaguer when torrential rain fell during the night and the desert turned into a morass so that we were up all night towing vehicles out back onto the road and even tanks were getting bogged. It really was chronic and then we got the order that we had to go back once more to Benghazi. We started to do this trip and when we got somewhere round about the Tocra Pass we had to turn round and go back again to Barce another 40 miles. This sort of order, counter-order, disorder was most demoralising in extremely unpleasant conditions because it was cold and wet and nobody knew what the hell was going on.

This on-off move forward, back, debacle carried on for about three or four days and we occasionally got the odd lift on tank transporters. Again, my diary shows that on 1st February there was a chronic flap and we stood to and covered something like 72 miles to Tobruk where we were promised there would be tank transporters to pick us up. There were but we were one tank transporter short and guess who was told he would have to motor on his tracks as far as possible and he would be picked up eventually! My diary for 2nd February shows that my own tank motored 184 miles eastward in about 20 hours, eventually reaching the Regiment's camp somewhere near Hellfire Pass; right on the frontier again. This meant that my driver and I shared spells of duty at the controls and I know that I fell asleep whilst driving and he most certainly did. When we finally got back to the Regimental rendezvous the distance covered apparently was a record then for a tank motoring on its tracks and I know that I damned well nearly fell asleep whilst reporting to the Adjutant because I was completely and utterly knackered.

We had a few days of well earned rest, though this consisted of getting refitted with 'fresh' tanks and, once again, knocking into shape new crews and general reorganising. A rather odd thing happened on February 8th, which was my birthday, which may sound very silly to readers. We got hold of our ration of whisky and beer and decided to have a small birthday party in the Squadron Mess, which consisted of the canvas top of a 3-ton lorry just sitting on the desert sand and we invited our CO over to have a celebration drink.

The whisky we used to get from the NAAFI varied enormously and the brand we then had was Lambs - rather more famous for their rum - and each bottle had a little plastic lamb as a label round the bottle neck. In 'B' Squadron we always felt that if there was any dirty work going then we were the Squadron to have to do it, so the Squadron Officers proudly wore these little lambs hanging from their battle-dress top pocket - "like lambs being led to the slaughter."

The beer came up in small tins, rather like the ones we have today, but they did not have the present day peel-off tops. The only way one could pour the beer out was to stand-by with the glass, or mug, very close to it and very quickly punch two holes in the top, hoping to decant it directly into said glass - if you only punched one hole then the beer came out in a terrific stream.

Unfortunately, on getting Frankie, our CO, his beer I only punched one hole and the beer hit him right smack in the face. Quite unintentional I assure you! He seemed to take this reasonably well at the time but shortly afterwards he said that he had an announcement to make and he said he was ordering us to remove our little lamb labels because he said, "You are too damned Squadron conscious, creating a precedent, so from now on you don't wear your lambs." In the cold light of day that sounds absolutely ridiculous but that silly little incident rankled with us for quite some time.

We got onto tank transporters once more and once again we started moving west past the old names: Mersa Matruh, Fort Capuzzo - along the Trigh Capuzzo - to El Adem and further on to Point 129 where we had a nasty aerial attack and eventually ended up at a place called Sigfht el Sidra.

Here, somewhere around about this area, on February 25th a very pleasant thing happened to me indeed. I was told that an officer had turned up in a truck and wished to speak to me in the mess, the mess once again being the top of a 3-ton lorry in the sand. When I went across to the mess who should be there but my elder brother Gerald who was with the RASC and God bless him, he had found out where we were and had turned up in his truck and he had a crate of beer with him. This was absolutely magnificent because rations were very tight and he was made an honorary member of the mess for life after that! We managed to meet up on various different occasions in the desert and after Alamein when we, the 8th Tanks, went up into Palestine and Syria, brother Gerald carried on with the 8th Army's triumphant westward move going right through Tripoli and Tunis and then across to Sicily and then into Italy and we met up again in Italy in 1944/5 on various different occasions.

Truth is stranger than fiction, as when the war ended in Italy on May 2nd 1945 we were both eventually flown back to England. We flew back on the same day, in the same flight and landed at the same aerodrome, Peterborough and we met up with one another in the Officers' Mess. Scores of others were frantically trying to use the few telephones available so we walked outside, about two miles or so away, found a telephone box and got through to our respective wives and our mother to tell them we were back safe and sound. At first my mother was angry when I spoke to her as she thought it was my brother fooling about and pretending to be me as she couldn't quite believe that we were both together. When she did realise this she just burst into tears.

Whilst we were not right up forward at this stage we were still near the sharp end and though our Valentines were slow, being infantry tanks, and not like the Crusader boys who could do about 25 mph or the Honey chaps who could crack along at about 30 mph or more, we still used to go out on armoured reconnaissance to find out where the Jerries were and what they were up to. We would then try and entice them out to battle, hoping to lure them to attack and chase us, and then we would turn about and try and lead them back onto our 25-pdrs and anti-tank guns because at long last we had learnt that this was the correct way to fight them in the desert, being armed only with our useless and hopeless 2-pdr. Sometimes this was successful and sometimes it wasn't.

Life was reasonably pleasant here as we were not under any undue strain or stress and by now we were desert veterans. We were well and truly acclimatised and accustomed to desert life and we had been battle tested and tried. The heat, the dust, the flies, the acute shortage of water and lack of fresh fruit and vegetables were all something that we were able to put up with and it seemed quite a normal sort of existence - we were true "Desert Rats."

The official water ration was a gallon per man per day (but what a hope) as our water came up to us in four-gallon tin containers and they used to leak like ruddy sieves so that we were very lucky indeed to get anything more than five to six pints per man, if that, and this was, of course, for all purposes. By that I mean radiators had to be topped-up first of all, then the remainder was needed for drinking, cooking, washing of self and then clothes and that was the order of preference. It is very difficult nowadays to imagine or even believe how we managed to cope with this meagre amount in the heat of the desert but somehow we did.

The Germans, on the other hand, had a magnificent container which we called a 'Jerry can.' This was a four-gallon metal container with a cap and strong handles and it was the most prized item of loot that one could get hold of and one of the first things when over-running any German positions was to get hold of as many 'Jerry cans' as possible. They really were quite a splendid piece of equipment.

Another innovation the Jerries had was their bread. This was dark brown and very nutritious and was individually sliced and each slice was wrapped in cellophane which made it very easy to dish out. Our bread, however, was the long rectangular loaf, or even a cobb loaf, and frequently covered in filth and flies and smelling of petrol or diesel and to try and ration out the amount of bread per man when there were nine men in a Troop and, say, four loaves was damn difficult.

The Italians were not quite so efficient as the Germans but their tinned tomatoes, vegetables and spaghetti were very useful to augment our rations, to say nothing of their bottles of Chianti and vino.

Believe it or not, but it is quite true, that on more than one occasion, when over-running their rear or more static positions we came across lorries which were full of cosmetics, stockings, women's underwear and all sorts of feminine things because it seemed that in the rear areas the Italians had sort of travelling brothels going around. Certainly the Powers-that-be with us had no truck with that sort of thing at all. More's the pity!

Mail was coming up pretty regularly and my wonderful wife, God bless her, wrote to me pretty well on an average of about three times a week throughout the entire war and her letters were a touch of sanity and fresh air in the rather crazy world that I was living in at that time. However, one felt that this lull, as it were, was not going to last for very long and that something was brewing and My God! it certainly was.

Somewhere about March 15th we were told to fit an extraordinary device to our tanks called a Sunshield. These were brown hessian stretched over tubular frames to fit onto the tanks so that from the air they would look like transport and on the ground, at a distance, they would also look like lorries. Apparently one of our Squadrons, I think it was 'C' Squadron, used these quite effectively going out and pretending they were lorries swanning about and when attacked by German armoured car patrols, or a small force of tanks, then dropping these sunshields and opening up with everything they had - much to the consternation of the Jerries. However in 'B' Squadron we were told to fit them and leave them in place and do nothing about it - so we knew that something was brewing up.

A few days later we were told that 'B' Squadron was going out on a special Column, with sunshields in situ, and that this Column was going to consist of a mixed bag of lorried infantry, a battery of towed 25-pounder guns, some Bofors ack-ack guns, two troops of anti-tank guns, two troops of armoured cars and ourselves (16 tanks) and that we were going to create a diversion behind the enemy lines.

What we were not told, however, was the reason for this which was that Malta was in desperate straits with its civilian population almost starving, being bereft of food, cooking oil and most other main essentials as convoy after convoy had not been able to get through. Accordingly a very big effort was going to be made to get another convoy through in the immediate future so the 8th Army was to stage diversionary attacks in the desert to draw off the attention of the Luftwaffe. In other words, our Column, together with a few others, were to act as aircraft bait.

So on the late afternoon of March 20th we all formed up and moved off into the blue. There had been very slight rain a day or two earlier, with a heavy dew at night, and the dun desert had miraculously changed colour as there were masses of lovely little blue and yellow flowers as far as the eye could see. They looked marvellous and it seemed an absolute sacrilege to me to have this damn column of tanks, guns, lorries, trucks, etc. crushing them, as they were not going to last for very long anyway.

We moved off more or less south/south-west from our assembly area to get well away from the main army positions and we were eventually spotted by a German reconnaissance plane. Shortly afterwards we heard the dreaded rumble and drone of aircraft and looked up to see about 20/25 Messerschmidt 110 fighter bombers with an escort of about 15 ME109 fighters and they circled over us a couple of times. The fighters then split up left and right and disappeared out of sight and then down came the 110's, one after the other, dropping their bombs and firing cannons.

Everybody in the Column opened up with everything they had, I would think even including revolvers, and at the very same time as this lot were coming down from the front of the Column the German fighters came in at absolutely deck level, at about 250 mph, firing their cannon and machine-guns at each flank. Tank turrets (certainly mine was) were operating on full power firing Besa at the maximum rate of fire of 1,200 rounds a minute in all directions and it was miraculous that we didn't shoot each other to pieces. They did a couple of attacks like this and then circled over us once more just to see what damage they had done and cleared off. The damage was not too bad, one or two trucks had been hit, and my gunner swore blind that he had hit a 110 smack on the nose with his 2-pdr at about 800 yards range as it was coming straight for us. I expect he was one of about 20 people who said the same thing because the fighter-bomber certainly veered off with smoke coming from it.

The Column Commander had told us earlier, much to our surprise, that our objective was Mechili Aerodrome. This caused us to raise our eyebrows as Mechili Aerodrome was a good 20 miles behind the German lines which meant that we were going in very deeply and obviously when we had attacked the damn place we were going to have a hell of a job getting out, so we knew it was going to be a pretty hairy operation.

However, after this aerial attack he wisely decided that as we had been spotted and that our position would be known to the Jerries our first objective was not going to be a suitable target so he decided to go for a secondary target, which was a small place called Eleut El Eleima. This was a small mound in the desert which the Germans had turned into a bit of a strong-point and it stuck out like a pimple on one's behind.

From then onwards this target and this particular scrap was always known as The Pimple.

We moved all night and stopped just before dawn and the armoured cars who were with us reported back that we were right behind the enemy and almost on top of The Pimple itself, but that they seemed to be quite unaware we were there.

The Column Commander decided to do an attack immediately and it was an absolute classic textbook attack with tanks, guns and infantry working in 100% co-operation. The Squadron moved out at once in line-ahead formation whilst the gunners put down a furious six minute bombardment all on and around The Pimple and we then turned in line formation with three Troops up. I was on the extreme right with my Troop and with George in the centre behind with two Troops in reserve. We went in, right at the foot of the barrage, which then lifted as the gunners plastered the centre of The Pimple with smoke as well as HE and the infantry were coming up close behind us in Bren-gun carriers and lorries.

Dawn had just about broken by then and as I came through the smoke, rather slowly, I saw about 40-45 yards away to my immediate right a German 50mm anti-tank gun facing away from me so I ordered my driver to swing right and my gunner to blast it with Besa machine-gun fire and the bloody gun jammed!! By this time we were about 30 yards away and the German anti-tank gunners had heard and seen us and all three of them were frantically trying to lift their gun around to face us and I could see them shouting and yelling at each other to do this. I then yelled to my gunner to fire the 2-pdr which he did and - there was a click - as we had a mis-fire...! The only one I had ever had in hundreds of rounds fired...

So there we were, now a mere 20-25 yards away, looking straight down the barrel of the 50mm with both of our guns out of action whilst I was tearing my hands to pieces as I frantically tried to clear the machine-gun stoppage and with my head and shoulders, as usual, out of the turret.

At that range if it fired, or rather when it fired, it would go clean through us like a knife through butter and probably out the other side and half-way to Tunisia. So I yelled to my driver to go flat out and charge the bloody thing when, to my complete astonishment, the three German gunners jumped to one side with their hands held up.

This was very fortunate for me but most unfortunate for them because almost at the precise moment they did that I cleared the machine-gun stoppage and without giving any further orders to my gunner I pressed the trigger myself and just mowed them down. We then smashed over them with the tank and hit the gun with such a wallop that I was winded and temporarily knocked out as my ribs hit the edge of the turret with one hell of a whumph.

It was a highly successful action with few casualties to ourselves. We took about 130 prisoners and knocked out about five or six of these 50mm anti-tank guns and our engineers had a great time going round and blowing up their 105mm ammo and destroying the guns and various stores and equipment. We piled the Jerries into their own lorries, put them in the middle of the Column, and hared back home as fast as we could. We were attacked twice more by the Luftwaffe but, once again, there was very little damage and our usual barrage of fire and we felt very elated and pleased with ourselves when we got back and we celebrated the battle of The Pimple on more than one occasion.

Apparently the convoy did get through to Malta on this occasion and helped to relieve the food situation somewhat so the diversions the 8th Army staged paid off in this respect. However, this little party and the attack we did on Bardia together with the bitter fighting we had been through in the previous November and December were really nothing to compare with what was to come in May, June and July though, naturally, we were blissfully unaware of this.

A rotten thing then happened to us whilst up in this area about this time. All our tanks and vehicles were widely dispersed as a precaution against aerial attack and on this particular morning the ambulance had come up to collect some wounded men. Our Padre, Sam Kemble, had been talking to them and met me whilst walking back to his truck.

I suppose we were about 150 yards away from the ambulance when we both heard the drone of an aircraft and, on looking up, saw a Messerschmidt 109 fighter coming across low and fast from our lines and going westwards. He was only about 500 feet up and he dipped the nose of his plane slightly and opened up with both cannon and machine-gun fire on the ambulance which was, of course, clearly marked with large Red Crosses on the sides and on the top.

Tragically his raking fire set it alight and he just disappeared out of sight. We both ran back to see what help we could give but it was quite useless and I'm afraid only one or two had managed to scramble out and the others had bought it.

It was a murderous and totally unnecessary thing to do and how that pilot could possibly justify what he did - well that will never be known.

Shortly after this incident Sam was posted away to Jerusalem - whether he asked for it or whether it came through automatically, I don't know. I did meet him again after the war and he told me then that he was so shattered by this experience that for a time he totally lost faith in everything, in particular with his calling, and that it took him a long time to come to terms again with both life and religion.

*   *   *

Towards the end of March news swept round the Regiment which just electrified everybody because, after seven long arduous months in the desert, everyone was going to get five days leave right back in the Delta. We were to go off in batches of so many at a time and on March 30th my batch came up. Oh Boy...

We left camp at about nine o'clock in the morning and drove absolutely flat out the entire day and the entire night with teams of drivers taking over one after the other. My diary shows that we reached Alex at about six in the morning and we were in Cairo by about three in the afternoon the next day. What absolute bliss it was to get back to civilisation again and to revel in long hot baths and drink pints of cool beautiful beer and have hours of blissful sleep in clean beds and wake up feeling refreshed, putting on clean fresh clothes and then setting forth to enjoy the fleshpots. It was absolutely marvellous and I won't mention anything about the fair sex here because this is not the time and place but that was certainly indulged in.

As I have already mentioned, being on leave and enjoying the amenities and blessings of civilisation once more was absolutely marvellous and I thought, with some misgivings, of the very much more primitive way of life to which I was about to return - particularly with regard to our Desert Rose. This was a pretty ramshackle affair consisting of a rough wooden seat on a tin or box with brown hessian surrounding it for 'privacy.' This was, of course, when we were not up the sharp end - that was just the matter of a shovel, a toilet roll and a hike.

On my last night of leave, whilst at the Cecil Hotel in Alex, being, naturally the best one, I somehow got hold of some tools and spent a considerable time undoing and removing the beautiful mahogany seat and lid of the lavatory adjacent to my bedroom. This I triumphantly took back with me up into the blue as a present for 'B' Squadron.

Its fame quickly spread around and officers from the other Squadrons had to 'have a go' on it but alas some bastard pinched it soon after it was installed. I never did find out the perpetrator of this atrocious crime.

When returning from leave I picked-up a brand new Armourer Staff-Sergeant named Craig, straight out from England, who was to join us. We were then south and west of Tobruk, some 500-600 miles up in the blue, which took about two to three days by lorry. S/Sgt. Craig was just awed by the sheer vastness of the desert and our apparently casual way of life and he told me, much later, that he thought I was completely bonkers as I did not appear to use a map - certainly never looked at my compass. He thought that either we were completely lost and would die of thirst as we would never, ever be found or that we would be captured by the Germans.

I must confess that map-reading was never my best subject but in the desert we used recognised landmarks such as a crashed Stuka; a group of burnt-out vehicles; a heap of 40-gallon oil drums or a cairn of stones as an aid to our navigation. S/Sgt. Craig thought that everything was very hit or miss and far too casual for a long time before he, too, became acclimatised as a Desert Rat.

It all went too quickly of course and as soon as I was back with the Squadron again we were out once more, on April 12th, on Column to Rotunda Segnali, but nothing very much seemed to have happened and Jerry was lying very doggo. We knew that something was brewing up owing to the tremendous activities in our own rear areas and reports of the same activities going on behind the German-Italian lines.

The 8th Army defence line was running from Gazala on the coast about 30 miles west of Tobruk, pretty well due south down to Bir Hacheim, where the Free French were and the area generally was pretty heavily mined. The 1st South African Division were up north in the Gazala area and in the centre of our line was 50th Division, the Tyneside and Tees boys, and further south of them was 150 Brigade with the Free French down at Bir Hacheim. Behind this the main armour under 13 Corps was held back in reserve more or less in the centre, a little further south was 30 Corps, the 7th Armoured Division for further reinforcements and further units in Tobruk itself.

We, the 8th RTR (less 'A' Squadron who were detached and up at Gazala with the South Africans) were part of a Column called 'Stopcol.' This consisted of two squadrons of tanks, a 25-pdr gun regiment, a battalion of South African Infantry, two troops of anti-tank guns, ack-ack and Bofors guns and two troops of armoured cars. There were other similar columns operating and we were all to be used as Armoured Mobile Reserves to plug a gap when and if there was a break-through between the flanks of any particular divisions.

With hindsight both armies were ready to start an attack rather like a couple of heavyweight boxers about to enter the ring. From all accounts the 8th Army was to go into action on or around June 2nd. However, Rommel beat us to the count and decided to start moving on the night of May 27th, by which time we, I mean 'B' Squadron, were already in our battle positions and waiting for the word go.

Gazala

As long as I live I will never ever forget the morning of May 28th. At first light we had fanned out from our closed leaguer positions to our battle positions and, once again, I was on the extreme right flank of the Squadron. There was nothing in sight at all to my right or behind me and the Troop to my immediate left was spread out and a long way away as we were dispersed covering as much ground as possible. I could see that my Troop was in a very slight depression so I left my three tanks and walked forward about 100 yards or so to look over the rim.

The ground sloped away very gently and very slowly dropping, I suppose, about 20 odd feet over a distance of 100 yards or so. The rising sun was behind me and all the stones on the desert were beginning to sparkle as the sunlight hit them and for about a mile there was the ordinary scrubland desert which I now knew so well, but then there seemed to be a most extraordinary change: it looked as though somebody had drawn a line from the left to right horizons, and behind this line the desert had changed colour and was completely black. For a moment I was puzzled and then I thought, "Christ Almighty! that's the whole bloody Panzer Korps in front of me!" The desert was absolutely crowded with guns, tanks, armour, troops and vehicles of every possible description.

I was not in fact looking at the whole of the Afrika Korps but the 21st Panzer Division and accompanying troops and opposite them were

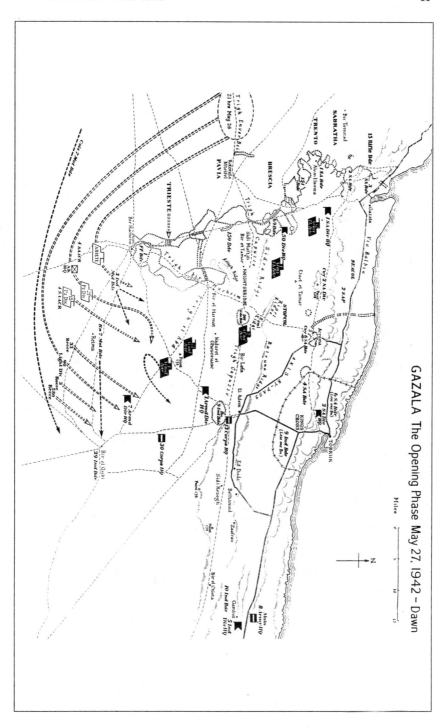

GAZALA The Opening Phase May 27, 1942 – Dawn

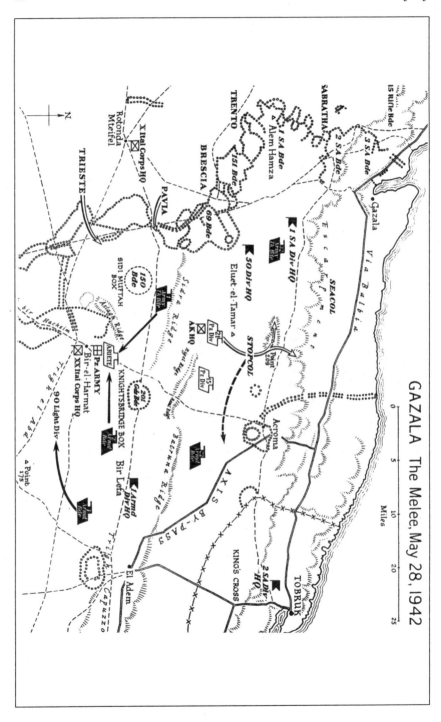

GAZALA The Melee, May 28, 1942

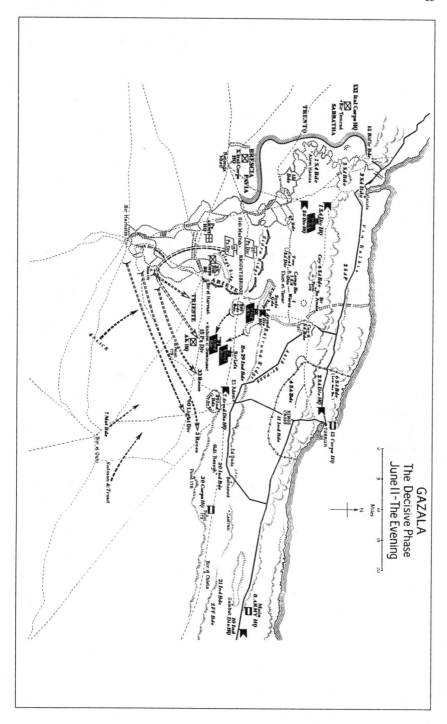

GAZALA
The Decisive Phase
June II-The Evening

just 16 tanks of 'B' Squadron with myself on the right and nothing else in sight! I rushed back to my tank and immediately reported to George on the radio what I had seen and straight away he came on the air and gave me strict instructions to stay where I was at all costs and that he and Berry ('C' Squadron) would try to rally on me as fast as possible but I was to stay put and not move.

I signalled for my tanks to move up towards me and for my Troop Sergeant and Corporal to join me and their comments, when I showed them what was in front of us, were similar to my own. Whilst we were talking and I explained what we had to do there was a roar of an engine behind us and we looked up and saw a Messerschmidt 110 flying very fast towards us and only about 20-30 feet up and we immediately threw ourselves flat on the deck. All he did however was to drop two orange marker flares and almost before these flares hit the deck I saw 40-50 black, squat shapes beginning to move out of the column and I thought, "Christ! this is it!" I ran back immediately to my tank and told George what was happening and, once again, he said, "OK stay where you are: be with you as soon as possible: out." Then of course all hell broke loose.

As I have already explained our 2-pdr gun was pretty useless at ranges of over 500 yards, whereas the German tanks could knock us out at twice that range, but I knew what it was like to experience the sound of solid shots screaming and tearing past one's head, also the nasty thud when hit hard. I therefore developed a technique with my gunner, calling it 'rapid fire' and taught my Sergeant and Corporal to do the same.

Normally, when the gunner fired, I was looking out the top with my binoculars observing his shot: instructing him either to alter his aim or distance: loading another round and getting him to fire a second shot: watching and observing once more. This would take about eight to ten seconds so that we would get off eight or ten rounds per minute. However, with 'rapid fire,' as soon as he got near the target I just slammed shells in as fast as I could as he continued firing with little or no correction. This method therefore meant that we would almost double our normal rate of fire and get off 15 rounds or more per minute.

As I had my Sergeant and Corporal doing just the same then there would be at least 25-35 shells per minute being fired and this could daunt the most intrepid tank commander trying to push forward fast and also give the impression that there were more than just three tanks opposing them.

Whilst waiting for George and Berry to rally on me and for the attack to commence I handed my binoculars to my driver to have a look at the situation for himself.

He was a quiet, stolid, dependable man who was very steady in action and a good driver and mechanic. I watched with some amusement as he lifted the glasses to his eyes to find out what his reaction would be - but I was totally unprepared for what then happened.

He looked, gasped slightly, gave a little shake of his body and then the front of his faded, dirty, khaki shorts turned a dark brown and I could see the urine trickling down his legs. I am sure that he was quite unaware of what he was doing so I quietly said, "You had better get back in and start up as things are going to be pretty hectic any moment now."

He handed the glasses to me and got back into his seat without saying a word and neither of us ever alluded to this incident and this is the first time that I have mentioned it to anyone.

We were in a good 'hull-down' position and as soon as the German tanks were about 800-900 yards away I gave my Troop the order to open up with 'rapid fire' and it is of interest to note that the wording of the citation for Sgt. Tilford's Military Medal, which he won that day, states "...his accurate and rapid fire prevented enemy tanks from outflanking us."

The advice and training with this method of fire certainly paid dividends that morning as it did give George and Berry time to get organised and to rally up alongside my Troop.

We had a very hectic scrap indeed which lasted for some considerable time but the sheer weight of numbers of the German Tanks, plus their artillery with 88's firing airbursts right over our heads, eventually forced us to give ground and pull back. The damned 88's were firing time-fused shells which burst about 20 feet above ground showering red-hot shrapnel in all directions and this caused Tank Commanders to keep well down in the turret as we had previously lost several chaps with wounds to head and shoulders in earlier actions from this type of attack. Our delaying action did, however, give our Column a chance to pull back and regroup in more favourable positions - at a price though as we lost 16 tanks out of 32 here.

This was one of the occasions when dear old George got himself knocked-out. He was well in front of most of us and on baling out he was heavily machine-gunned as he tried to run back, so I had to spin my tank around and go and pick him up. You will notice that I said "spin my tank around," because we had learnt by then - at least I had - that the best way of preventing oneself getting knocked out was by having the tank facing away from the battle. This was not negative thinking but because the armour of the engine covers was very thick (about three-and-a-half inches), and angled, so that shells hitting the engine casing direct would frequently ricochet straight off without penetrating. This also gave the tank an odd silhouette making it a much harder target to hit and damage was comparatively slight if so hit. It was also easier to manoeuvre the tank this way because I could tell the driver to "advance flat out" - meaning get the hell out of here and then do a crash stop some 50 yards or more away, thus confusing the German tank gunners aim, whilst loosing off a few quick rounds myself. Conversely, I could get my driver to reverse slowly thus shortening the range to my advantage. Also, if it was necessary to move to another position the tank did not have to swing broadside on and turn to get out of battle because my driver could then just put his foot down hard and get away. Furthermore, it was pretty disconcerting for the wretched driver sitting down in the front of the tank facing the action seeing shells and stuff shooting at him and wondering what on earth was going to happen with the next shot.

In an effort to hold ground and have some sort of focal strong point infantry brigades used to build what they called a Brigade Box. This consisted of laying out some mines and putting up some wire and then having the infantry in slit trenches forward supported with guns and anti-tank guns from the centre and the sides. Rather like an old sort of infantry square. The trouble was in this very confused fighting that armoured mobile columns such as ours were frequently called upon to go to the aid and rescue of a particular box and en route we would probably get embroiled in a tank battle, or by the time we got there we would find that the attack had been beaten off or that it was a complete false alarm or that the poor chaps had been overrun anyway and frequently, on such a move like this, no sooner had we got to the box than we would be recalled to go screaming back the way we had come. All very confusing and very, very tiring.

Somewhere about this time an odd thing happened to me. As I have previously mentioned we were then engaged in very heavy fighting for a continuous long period and were utterly exhausted as we could only manage to get about two to three hours sleep in any one period of 24 hours, sometimes not even that.

I had finished my one hour sentry duty and wireless watch and crashed out to sleep at the side of my tank with my two blankets and ground sheet and took off my revolver belt, with ammo pouch and compass, before I lay down, placing it beside me.

On being awakened for the usual dawn stand-to my belt, revolver and compass were missing. I checked with my crew but couldn't find it and shortly after daybreak we moved off. I simply couldn't understand what had happened to it.

The mystery was clarified for me, many months later, by my Troop Sgt., 'Ticker' Tilford MM. He was on leave from Palestine with another Sgt. E— from 'B' Squadron who was a very tough character who had also won an MM and who eventually left us to join the Long Range Desert Group. He was that sort of man.

They were sharing a room and Sgt. E— tipped out his kitbag at the bottom of which Sgt. Tilford saw a revolver belt complete with pouch and compass. He managed to check the number and realised it was mine! Sgt. E— grinned and said he could get a good price for it on the black market.

Having been badly burnt in training I was always terrified of being wounded and trapped inside a burning tank and swore that I would shoot myself if that happened - so its loss was of particular significance to me. A pretty rotten thing to do anyway.

My diary is very sketchy owing to the lack of time to do anything about it and I can see, for example, that on June 2nd I have got down "two more scraps at Tamar again one in the morning, one in the evening, both pretty heavy. Numbers 11 and 12," and I can only assume these must have been the 11th and 12th particular tank battles we had been in during that short period.

On June 6th I apparently left the Squadron on detachment to go to the 44th RTR who needed some reinforcements and I was under the command of an officer whom I will not name because I was so furiously angry with him for the way in which he handled my Troop. We went on what I described in my diary as "just a fighter sweep," which meant a small group of us, about seven or eight tanks of which my Troop of three was a part. We were put in the lead to go and swan around a particular area and told to knock out an Italian position which was well supported with guns and had quite a lot of transport.

We were getting fairly close and I came up on the air and said that I could see the transport and had opened fire and that we were being fired upon by anti-tank guns and artillery and asked where the hell he was? He came up on the air and said "It's OK Ham - we are right behind you" but when I looked round there was not a bugger in sight.

We knocked out the odd transport or two and put paid to one or two guns but we were getting fairly heavily clouted so I decided that discretion was the better part of valour and with no support at all I ordered the Troop to return to our rendezvous.

I was talking to Cpl. Clee and Sgt. Tilford whilst we were brewing up when suddenly, out of the blue, a single shell came whistling over, landing right in amongst us and blowing us all over. I got to my feet and dusted myself down but Sgt. Tilford was on his knees moaning, "I can't see - I can't see" whilst Cpl. Clee was lying on the ground gasping and breathing heavily and badly.

I couldn't see a mark on him at first but then I noticed a small tear in his khaki shirt. I ripped it open and there was a tiny little hole where a piece of shrapnel had gone smack into his heart and - as I held him - he gasped once more and died.

It was a damn shame as he was a magnificent bloke, an old Reservist, who was about to be promoted to sergeant and very popular both in the Troop as well as the Squadron. Sgt. Tilford had been temporarily blinded by the blast and concussion but I was completely untouched.

The 44th Tank bloke came back very pleased with himself saying Brigade were very pleased that we had shot the place up and when I explained what had happened to my Sergeant and Corporal he didn't seem to be very sympathetic and he was getting all the credit for the work we had done at the expense of my Corporal and my Sergeant. Fortunately I was able to rejoin my own Squadron later that evening.

The next day we had been out on a couple of similar sweeps and had pulled back in the early afternoon to refuel and to re-ammo. I was leaning against the side of a tank and talking to Cpl. Foyle, who was another fine Reservist and a good friend of Cpl. Clee. I was telling him what had happened the day before when suddenly there was the crack of an anti-tank gun being fired - a bang! and a flash, right in between us, as the AP shot hit the side of the turret.

Cpl. Foyle immediately collapsed with blood gushing out all over his face - once again I was splattered with it - and two others were slightly wounded from ricochets.

I looked round wildly to see where on earth it had come from and the only likely looking vehicle was a Marmon-Herrington armoured car about 300-400 yards away.

I half ran and walked over to it and angrily shouted out, "What the bloody hell did they think they were doing in opening fire on us?" They were a South African crew and the NCO commander looked startled and ducked down inside. I shouted out that they had seriously wounded one of my corporals and also wounded two other men. He then re-appeared and said, "Hell, man! It wasn't us and we have just been told to move off elsewhere," and off they went.

I was seething with anger and impotence but there was nothing that could be done about it - it was just another rotten and stupid mistake which so often happens in war. Unfortunately Cpl. Foyle died of his wounds and he was another damn fine man tragically wasted.

The armoured car had, I believe, a small 15-20mm gun and as they were the only other vehicle anywhere near us then it must have been them who fired. Whether the gunner fired by accident or design I just wouldn't know and it was just one of those inexplicable and stupid accidents which happens in the fog of war.

I think it is well worth quoting from *The Tanks* by Captain B.H. Liddell Hart about this particular period and this particular battle: "The Gazala battle had been a tremendous test of endurance for all who took part," and what it entailed for tank crews can be realised to some extent from the following extract from a detailed and dispassionate report of the medical research section at GHQ MEF in July 1942:

> Fatique in tank crews has been one of the major problems with the present campaign in Libya. This is attributed to the longer hours of daylight than in previous campaigns and to the more intense prolonged fighting.

> The following is a brief outline of the average tank crew's day. The men are wakened at 05.00 hrs i.e. before daylight and get into their tanks which they drive out of leaguer to battle or patrol positions which they reach by first light.

> Battles commonly occur in the early morning or in late afternoon or evening. In the middle of the day the heat haze is usually so great as to make accurate fire difficult. It is unusual for actual fighting to occupy

more than three of the daylight hours. The rest of the time is spent in alert watchfulness or patrolling and in waiting for or preparing for an attack.

It is universally agreed that these hours of expectancy are much more trying than the actual battle periods. Commanders have a particularly fatiguing time because in order to get immediate all round vision they keep their heads above the turrets. This necessitates their standing because tank seats as at present constructed cannot be adjusted to a height which allows them to sit.

Occasionally it may be possible for one or two of the crew to get out and stretch their legs or to 'brew-up' but it is not at all uncommon for the crew to remain in the tank for the whole of the daylight hours. Engine noise and fumes and gun fumes and the wearing of headphones all add to fatique.

It is usually 21.00 hrs or later at this time of the year before the opposing tanks gradually draw apart and finally seek their respective leaguers. This often necessitates two-three hours of night driving on the part of the tank crews in order to reach some signal point for the next day's battle. On reaching leaguer they must first refuel, load and stow away ammunition, a process which requires anything from 1 to 1½ or 2 hours and must then carry out minor repairs and general maintenance to the tank and distribute rations. It is rarely earlier then 00.30 hrs to 01.00 hrs when the men are at least able to get into their blankets. Nor is a day's work done yet because each man must stand an hour's guard. It is evident that three hours is the maximum sleep that can be obtained.

In the earlier days of the campaign when the moon was full frequent attacks were made by the enemy at night on our leaguers both from the air and by tanks on the ground. These attacks still further reduced the hours of rest and a number of officers have stated that they have gone 48 and even 72 hours without being able to get any sleep at all.

It is generally accepted opinion amongst Senior Regimental Officers interviewed that under conditions outlined above it is impossible for men to go on fighting with any degree of efficiency for more than a week and many would make the period even shorter. It has however been the policy in the present campaign to use troops until casualties prevents them functioning as a unit, at which juncture they are amalgamated with similarly depleted units. Some of these units have seen almost continuous fighting for almost 18-20 days. The opinion was expressed that experienced troops though exhausted were better than troops without battle experience.

It appears that some form of alteration to tank crews must be devised in order to ensure a necessary minimum of rest and recuperation especially for prolonged campaigns. It has been suggested that a 50% increase in the personnel of tank crews would enable units to alternate those crews that needed it most.

Each tank crew besides fighting and performing numerous duties briefly outlined above must prepare its own meals. Crews can cook only when they can leave their tanks and this is usually done only when they are in leaguer, and as noted above, they leave and return to leaguer during the hours of darkness when a strictly maintained blackout prevents the lighting of fires. The only opportunity for a hot drink is during the lull in the fighting in the daytime and as pointed out above this is often impossible.

Nights in the desert even in midsummer are cold enough to make it necessary to wear an overcoat: inability to get a hot drink before retiring, or at breakfast in the morning, is a great hardship.

Some units have tried sending up hot food in hay-boxes by night with a 'B' Echelon but this has not been successful. The food, having been cooked some 12-15 hours previously, is often cold and unpalatable on arrival. 'B' Echelon frequently does not arrive until after the men have retired when they would rather sleep than eat and, finally, it is not uncommon for the 'B' Echelon to fail entirely to appear for a day or two at a time.

In contrast with this state of affairs the German armoured units have a travelling Field Kitchen which is kept well forward and supplies the tank crews with a hot meal at night and a hot drink in the morning.

What the report does not state however is that we had then been up in the Desert for something like ten months and all the time without fresh vegetables, meat, fruit, etc. so that we were lacking, I would imagine, in certain vitamins. This caused a horrible thing called Desert Sores. One only had to bang an arm or leg against the tank, or gun, or something and break the skin and within 24 hours one would have a very unpleasant suppurating sore - rather like a boil. The only treatment available was to smother it with a cream or ointment which was a sort of purplish, gentian blue in colour and it was quite normal to see a man in old, faded shorts and dirty shirt, with his beret on the back of his head, with both his hands bandaged and bandages on one or both knees and spots of purple, blue patches. I even had a sticking plaster on my classic nose where I had cracked it on the edge of the turret. These boils were damn sore and they certainly helped to pull one down in spirit and feel pretty miserable.

We, the 8th RTR, were almost continuously in action from the morning of May 28th until we were finally pulled out, at the El Alamein box, on July 13th, i.e. a period of just over six weeks. There were occasions, of course, when we were so depleted of tanks and crews that we were temporarily pulled back, some 40 miles or so, to a Tank Reinforcement area where we picked up 'fresh' tanks and crews. We had only about 48 hours or so to get them into shape and then went back straight in again as the situation was so desperate. This happened possibly two or three times during this six week period so we could truthfully say that we were continuously in action for approximately five whole weeks. By the time we had got back to The Alamein Box we were just like walking zombies and I don't think that I have ever been so completely and utterly exhausted and tired, both physically and mentally, in my life. It is difficult to describe the state we were in - to put it bluntly - completely bloody knackered.

One thing the report in Captain Liddell Hart's fine book *The Tanks* (Volume II) did not mention was the fact that the whole month of June was, in itself, the worst possible period to be in the actual desert because of the misery of the Khamsin Wind.

At this time of the year the pressure built up down in the south of the Sahara so that a hot wind started blowing up to north, i.e. to the coast and as it moved at about 15-20 mph it picked up dust and sand all the time. I don't know the actual temperature but it must have been well over 110°F and it was like being in a thick, hot, pea-soup fog. You just could not see your hand in front of your face and the cursed sand got into every single orifice in the body. It got into the eyes, the nose, mouth, ears, anus... It got into the engine, it got into the guns, it got into the wireless set, it really was incredible. It would blow for about two days and nights and then stop for about a day. Then the cursed thing would start up once more and this went on for four to five weeks, non-stop, right through June and into July.

There was absolutely nothing that one could do about it and we just had to try and exist and endure this ghastly Khamsin misery - and we even had to fight in the ruddy thing. It was sheer hell. To try and live with it was bad enough but to have to fight in it... well, it defies description.

Two very bizarre incidents happened during this Khamsin period, one of which was humorous - the other horrendous.

We had moved up one morning but about mid-day we just had to stop because we couldn't see where the hell we were going. The crews were huddled up exhaustedly at the sides of their tanks with one or two adventurous spirits trying to 'brew up' inside, which was quite illegal and highly dangerous but frequently done. I then heard, above the sound of the wind, a most extraordinary noise, a mixture of moaning, bellowing and thudding and I simply couldn't make it out at all. The sandstorm then momentarily lifted and when it did a roar of laughter went up from the crews because there - about 20 or so yards away - was a damn great bull camel trying hard to have his way with a female camel and she didn't seem to be enjoying it at all!

Each time she tried to get up from under him, off the ground, with a mighty swing from his powerful neck he would crash her sideways and down again and when he tried to mount her - well! - the size of his old what-not was like a ruddy great telegraph-pole! To the cheers and roars of the crews he at last had his way with this wretched camel. She still didn't seem to appreciate what was happening and kept turning round, snarling and biting his chest and forelegs and he would equally snarl and smash her down again with his ruddy great neck. It really was a most disgusting sight and I couldn't help thinking that here we were, in this foul, filthy desert and here were these foul, filthy animals procreating in this foul, filthy way in this foul, filthy sandstorm - it just didn't make any sense at all!

The other occasion, which was about a day later, was a very different story altogether.

We had moved up and, once again, all movement stopped in the afternoon because of this incredible sandstorm and I was sitting in the turret of my tank, drooped over the gun, with my head resting on my arms and I was simply so tired, exhausted and utterly fed-up that I just didn't care a damn what happened to me - whether I was killed, wounded, taken prisoner, whatever. All I wanted to do was to get the hell out of this cursed, bloody desert.

As I have already mentioned, the wind was blowing at about 15-20 mph and one could hear it moving across the desert whipping up the scrub and small stones and moaning over the tank when, quite suddenly, I lifted my head, looked up and jumped to my feet, saying, "Christ! What's happened?" because all sound of movement had suddenly stopped - just like that.

When I looked out of the turret, whereas the sandstorm had been blowing hard from left to right - i.e. from south to north to the coast - this movement had now stopped and I could see the sand and dust retreating away from me and falling almost vertically. The next moment there was the most wonderful cool breeze, at least it seemed cool anyway, and the sandstorm started moving again only this time it was going from right to left, in the opposite direction. "Thank God!" I thought "the blasted Khamsin has finished!" as this was the cool air coming in off the sea and blowing all this foul sand away. It was absolutely miraculous and the relief was simply wonderful but, unfortunately, this relief was very short lived indeed.

I suppose we only mustered about 12-14 tanks in a small huddle and suddenly, when the sand storm cleared away, we saw right in front of us, no more than 900 yards away, about 40 or more squat Panzer III's and IV's. In other words a German tank force had been coming up to meet us but they had had to stop as well and at that range, out-gunning us and out-numbering us by at least by two or three to one, well they could make mincemeat out of us. But that wasn't all, what was far worse was that in between them and us, in fact I would say closer to the German tanks, was a complete British supply column of soft vehicles. I suppose there must have been about 25 or 30 of them crammed full of petrol, ammunition, men, rations and so on and almost as one gun all those German tanks opened up with everything they had and the carnage was just terrible. We naturally opened fire ourselves so that these wretched chaps in the lorries and trucks were caught in the crossfire of about 60 tanks all blazing away at one another.

I could see trucks going up left, right and centre all over the place and one lorry trying to turn and being hit broadside by another and overturning with men scrambling out and running away and then a 1500 cwt truck came roaring towards me at about 40 mph and I can see the driver now. He was bare-headed, his shirt was open down to his waist and flapping out behind him in the breeze. He was swinging the wheel left and right, driving on a zig-zag course, and his mate was hanging on for grim life as they bumped and banged about - and they were towing a quad behind full of ammunition. The were only about 15 yards away and almost alongside me and to my right when they got a direct hit and the whole thing just blew up in an almighty explosion of flame and smoke and both the driver and his mate were thrown out on fire. There was absolutely nothing I could do to help them as we were firing just as fast as I could slam in shells. The smoke was totally obscuring my tank and the ammunition was going off in all directions and my driver thought we had been hit and was ready to bail out. I yelled to him get the tank moving the hell out of here and we pulled away most certainly firing on the move this time. I then saw a chap who was running and waving and then going flat on his face as he was being heavily machine-gunned. He was about 300 yards away so we swung round and rushed to pick him up.

He was a Gunner Major called Loder-Symmonds of, I think, the 4th RHA and as he scrambled up on the back he breathlessly said, "For God's sake get me back to by Battery" so he could give us some fire support, because his truck with his wireless set had been hit. I was loading and firing the gun like mad and said, "I haven't got the bloody time to do that and I can't pull out," so he asked me to try and get in touch with his Battery on my set. Again I had to say I was too damn busy as we were firing for all we were worth with the tank rocking on its suspension with our rate of fire and bucking every now and then as we heard the thuds when being hit hard. Stuff was simply flying in all directions and it was a very tough scrap indeed.

He then yelled out, "Where's your Squadron Commander?" and I looked irritably and pointed vaguely, "Over there, pennants flying, about 200 yards away." "Can you get me to him?" he bellowed once more. "OK I'll do that" and off we went still firing away. "What's his name?" and I answered "Sutton, George Sutton."

At this he looked a bit surprised and asked, "Has he got a nickname - Snakebite?" "Yes, he has," I replied equally surprised. "My God! I knew him then in Malaya. He was, damn it, one of the rubber planters," and I thought, "Oh my God not one of those!" We drew up alongside and George, as usual head and shoulders out of his turret, looking a bit surprised to see me there and this RA bloke jumped onto his tank and this is absolutely true, it was really like something out of a Noel Coward play, because Loder-Symmonds held out his hand and said, "Hello George old boy, fancy seeing you here" and George, who had a very loud voice bellowed out, "Good God Almighty! Bob, what the fucking hell are you doing up here?" and Loder-Symmonds said, "Well I suppose the same as you, a bit of a party, what." I thought, "Oh my God let's get the hell out of here and get on with the battle!"

Again somewhere around about a day or two later the remnants of our two Squadrons, probably about six or seven tanks, had linked up with a similar number of Grant tanks, I think of the Queen's Bays, and we were at the foot of a very slight escarpment and gradually being picked off one by one by superior German forces.

The Queen's Bays suddenly pulled out because, I believe, they were completely out of ammunition, which left about four of us, and

Reggie's tank had been hit badly and was crawling up to the top of the escarpment and I looked round and realised I was the only one down at the bottom so decided it was better if I got up onto the top as well. I got into a hull down position when I got up there and I found I was the only one because everybody else had gone further back still. I then heard a frantic radio call from Berry Veale, one of the Squadron Commanders (later to be a Lieutenant-Colonel with a DSO, MC, and I think he commanded the 9th RTR with the Guards Armoured Division in Germany) calling out for everybody to join him and get back as fast as possible to the top of the escarpment to join the lone tank which was up there. I looked round and saw a solitary tank moving up and the Tank Commander was waving and of course it was good old George Sutton and between the two of us we hung on until the rest of them joined us - only about eight or ten of them - and we stayed up there until dark, holding the Jerries back, and then had to pull back once more into leaguer torefuel and re-ammo.

The next day the same sort of thing happened and I heard something on the wireless which was very tragic indeed.

We were engaged with a similar number of German tanks in a hectic scrap so we couldn't do anything to help. About two miles away, to the north of us, was one of these infantry boxes, the Worcester Box I believe, and this was absolutely true as I heard it quite clearly on my tank radio set.

Apparently they were being heavily shelled and attacked by a strong German Tank force and a very young, nervous voice came up on the air, saying, "Hello Beer, this is Beer 3. German tanks about 1,000 yards. What shall I do?" Dead silence. A few moments later a more anxious voice came on the air again saying, "Hello Beer! this is Beer 3. German tanks about 600 yards. Please what shall I do? Over." Almost immediately after that a frantic voice, "Hello Beer! Beer 3. German tanks only 400 yards. What shall I do? Over." Back came a beautifully calm English voice, saying, "Hello Beer 3. Beer here. I would think a very good range to open fire. Out."

Unfortunately that Box was overrun with pretty heavy casualties and the rest taken prisoner. It was very sickening, hearing this, and being quite unable to help or do anything about it.

My diary shows sketchy entries, such as June 14th: 'terrific tank battle at Point 208 this morning (14)' and then 'destroyed Mk. III' followed by the entry 'another heavy ruddy scrap this evening (15)' and for the life of me I cannot remember the exact details of how we knocked-out that Panzer III but certainly I would not have put it in my diary if we hadn't done so. I seem to remember having caught it from the rear and in the flank.

With reference to the above diary entry 'another ruddy heavy scrap in the evening (15)' - indeed it was.

We had had a hell of a scrap with tanks at Point 208 that morning and had pulled back to regroup, but the Khamsin dust had made it impossible to do anything more until about 7pm that evening.

Once again, we were a small group of 12-15 tanks of both 'B' and 'C' Squadrons and I was away on the right flank, which seemed to be my usual position, with nothing else in sight. I was very, very tired and hoping like hell that nothing else would happen that day - but what a hope.

I suddenly saw a cloud of dust approaching me at a very fast rate and, raising my binoculars, saw it was a Honey tank doing about 30 mph or more - in other words going like the proverbial clappers. It did a crash stop alongside me, bucking on its suspension like a bucking bronco, and an artillery captain who was an FOO (Forward Observation Officer) yelled, "You'd better get the hell out of here and fast - as there are about 50-60 Mark III's and IV's coming right behind me" and with that he shot off flat out. "Oh! Christ! Here we go again," I thought and reported to George on the wireless. As usual he told me to stay put and that he would bring up the rest of the others to me.

Once again it was a question of waiting - and praying - and then "OK - rapid fire - let them have it."

Somehow or other we did manage to hold them back until nearly dark and the FOO must have got back in time because we did get some good artillery support this time, but it was a very heavy scrap and we lost several tanks up here.

The Cauldron

Shortly after this little party I was detached with six tanks to join up with the Guards Brigade at Knightsbridge in The Cauldron area and it was a very rough do indeed. In the evening I went over to the adjutant of either the Queen's Bays or another cavalry crowd, in his Crusader tank, to say that we were very low on ammunition and fuel. "Can't help you there old boy! We use petrol and not diesel. You'll have to sort it out yourself."

It was a very grim situation, nobody knew where anyone else was or just what was happening and it was a question of 'devil take the hindmost.' Quite how I found a) diesel and b) my own crowd I just cannot remember and I am probably posted still as a deserter!

Again around about this time, maybe two or three days later, we had a very heavy and hectic day once more with several scraps and then we got involved in a fierce tank battle about 8.30-9.00pm and, as usual, we were outnumbered and outgunned and being picked off left, right and centre.

I saw a tank on my left being hit and going up in flames and its commander jumped out and started running towards me. It was Peter Kitto of 'C' Squadron so we spun round and went and picked him up. He scrambled up on the back and as we pulled back, firing over our tail, he was standing over the driver's hatch with his back to the way we were going.

Suddenly I just went completely berserk. I ordered my driver to halt and started 'rapid fire' and my gunner, a chap called McBean who was a South African and a damned good shot, was firing as fast as I could load until he started shouting out that he couldn't see a target as we were kicking up so much dust and smoke from our rate of fire. Apparently I was yelling, "I don't care a bugger! Fire, damn you, fucking well fire..." I was completely beside myself with anger and rage until I felt a hell of a pain on the top of my head and, as I came to, I found it was Peter Kitto thumping me with his clenched fist as hard as he could, shouting out, "For Christ's sake Ham! Pull out you stupid bastard. PULL OUT!"

When I looked up and out I said, "My God! Driver advance flat out" because there were 12 or more German tanks only about 300-400 yards away all blazing away at me and when we pulled back into the small leaguer area of the remnants of the two Squadrons, some way back, the men gave us a ragged cheer and said they couldn't understand how I had not been knocked out as apparently I was in a cone of fire with tracer from the AP shells (armour piercing) going all around the top of the turret, round the sides, hitting the ground and going through the suspension, ricocheting off the tank, etc. and it really was a miracle that we were not hit and knocked out.

We were all very, very tired by then and very few in numbers with several wounded, one of whom was Hickey Sugden (MC and Bar) with a smashed arm in a blood-stained sling. He looked very rough, and no wonder as it was a nasty wound. His tank had been penetrated and his gunner killed at his side. We hung on there until about midnight with German patrols getting very close and Verey lights going up all over the place. We had orders to stay put as long as possible and keep them at bay and then to pull back very slowly as it was essential to keep this last corridor into Tobruk open for as long as possible.

When we were eventually given the order to pull back, Brian McCabe, our adjutant (MC and Bar), came running across to me saying that his tank had slid into a slit trench and was embedded with a roll of barbed wire all around the tracks - and could I help pull him out. So we tried to do this and I can't remember where I got hold of some wire-cutters, but I did, and frantically started cutting this damned wire from the tracks and suspension. Every now and then there was the thump of mortar shells, machine-gun bursts etc. and Brian was saying, "For Christ's sake Ham! Get a move on or we will both end up in the bloody bag" and his gunner and mine were firing long bursts of Besa machine-gun to keep the Jerries at bay. At last we got the blasted tracks clear and pulled out at the last possible moment. It was extremely hairy and I really thought that we had had it as the Jerries were so bloody close.

We then had to hold open this corridor into Tobruk and when we at last got the order to move in ourselves, about four o'clock in the morning, I was one of many who were just falling dead asleep, standing up in the turret. It really was chronic as we were all utterly exhausted, both physically and mentally.

One incident, which I remember clearly but which is chronologically out of place, happened two or three days before we had the tough job of holding open the corridor back into Tobruk. As I have said before, we repeatedly seemed to be outnumbered by German tanks and on this particular day we had already had two or three scraps and then had to pull back to refuel and re-ammo. It was about 6pm and we leaguered close to remnants of the 4th RTR, who were also equipped with Valentines at that time.

We were just about getting down to a welcome meal when there was a cloud of dust as we saw the 4th move off and thought, thank God! It's them and not us again. However George then came running through, jumping onto his tank and shouting out, "Start up! Mount! We are off and joining in with the 4th." "Oh my God! Here we go again," I thought.

As we moved off he came up on the wireless and said that we were going in to break up a German counter-attack and were to follow the 4th wherever they went. There were about 15 of them, and we were about the same so for the first time for ages there were 30 of us for this attack and we certainly knocked hell out of the Jerries on that occasion and put paid to his counter-attack.

The one thing that I remember particularly about this party was that Sgt. Tilford MM had come back because his eyes were OK and he nearly took the top of my head off as he fired at something straight over the top of my turret from about ten yards behind me and the blast of his ruddy gun - well that started the severe deafness I have suffered from ever since the end of the war. My diary also contains a few days later a cryptic note saying, 'fired 132 rounds today,' and I certainly remember telling Leslie 'Doc' Milton about that time of the excruciating earache I was getting each time the gun fired. All he could do was to give me some aspirins and a good slug of medicinal brandy.

It may be noticed that I frequently mention 'B' and 'C' Squadrons but hardly ever talk about 'A' Squadron. This is because 'A' Squadron were, at that time, away and attached to the South African Division at Gazala. This sort of thing constantly happened - a Squadron being away on detachment - so that we hardly ever fought as a complete Regiment, which of course we should have done.

About the only times I can remember when we were all together were in our first action at Sidi Rezegh, in November 1941, which didn't last for very long, and again in the attack on Bardia. The 8th Army command in those days never seemed to grasp the essential principle of concentration and of a real concentration of force in one particular place. We were forever being used in 'penny packets,' instead of grouping a large tank force and smashing the enemy in a particular area or battle.

Rommel however did just this and in *The Rommel Papers* edited by Captain Liddell Hart it states that although he was outnumbered in tanks by nearly three to one he gratefully accepted our battle strategy of attacking him, so often, with only one armoured brigade at a time. As his tanks had heavier guns he invariably inflicted heavy losses on us and thus made us pay very dearly for using these tactics. Even in Italy, some two years later, this attitude still persisted and as we, the 7th Armoured Brigade, were an independent brigade we were thus 'parcelled out' to any infantry division which wanted tank support. We rarely got to know our infantry or gunners well, as we would have liked, and should have done, since we worked with so many different units.

Consequently a single squadron would be attached to an infantry battalion and one had to protest vigorously when the infantry CO would try to split the squadron up having a Troop to an infantry company, etc. I used to argue that it was essential to keep the Squadron together for maximum fire support and mutual self protection in the dangerous and difficult Italian countryside. Not that I always got my way though and it was hard, as a major, having to argue with colonels and sometimes brigadiers of both infantry and gunners.

We seemed to pick up a few more tanks in dribs and drabs here and there but we never were able to muster more than about ten or twelve at the very most on our own. At that time we were constantly doing a rearguard from Tobruk, back to Capuzzo, The Wire and eventually right back into Egypt itself. It was very tiring, frustrating and demoralising as we never had any proper co-operation with other tank regiments, infantry or guns and it always seemed to be just a small group of us - on our 'Jack Jones' as it were - as if we were the only ones left to do any fighting.

There was one incident just south of Capuzzo when Reggie Campbell's tank had been hit and I was alongside trying to help when we saw a Panzer Mark IV, which had a 75mm gun, about 1200-1500 yards away and so completely out of range for our wretched 2-pdr and we wondered what the hell it was doing - or going to do. We soon learnt because as I was talking to Reg the bastard fired and it was a splendidly accurate shot. He was at the side of my tank and I was leaning out over the turret and the damn shell landed right at his feet, knocking him over, and blowing me back down inside. Luckily he was not hurt and jumped up and when he saw me lying down at the bottom of the turret he was worried in case I had been hit. Most fortunately I was also unhurt and only temporarily concussed by the blast. It really was a magnificent shot and we were furious we could not retaliate.

As his tank had been knocked out he suggested that I should put it completely out of action so we fired at the engine a couple of times from only about 20 yards range. We saw his Valentine judder and jump but there was no smoke from it and I guessed that we had penetrated and put the engine out of action.

However, we managed to recover the damn thing a few hours later and, to our horror and disbelief, found that even at that point blank range the bloody 2-pdr had not penetrated. Either the armour was very good indeed (which it was) or the 2-pdr was completely and utterly bloody useless (which it was).

We told George about this and he insisted that we were not to tell anyone else in the Squadron because that would be very demoralising as the situation was very bad - the news had just come through that Tobruk had fallen again. This was really grim and meant that we were back to square one once more.

We hung around in this general area for another day or so doing the usual rearguard stuff and once again dear old George got himself knocked-out and I was at hand to pick him up for the second time. It was shortly after this that he damaged his hand so severely that he had to be sent back out of action for good.

A rather amusing incident then occurred in this area when we were somewhere south of Capuzzo and came across a huge supply dump - one of many scattered in these rear areas. It was simply marvellous getting in amongst it and the tank crews were, quite naturally, helping themselves to everything on hand. Unfortunately my immediate area seemed to consist of almost nothing other than tons of tinned fruit, beans, bully, etc. and we searched high and low for whisky, cigarettes and the like but getting only a little of these highly prized bits of loot.

Suddenly there was a cloud of dust and a small truck came roaring up to me and when it stopped out jumped a young and pale looking NAAFI Officer. He was furiously angry and asked what the hell did we think we were doing as we had no authority or indents to take stores like this and that we were to put it all back.

"For Christ's sake man!" I exploded "There's about ten square miles of the bloody stuff here, so what the hell do you expect. Anyway Jerry is right on our tail. Do you expect us to leave it to him!" But he was still furious and insisted that we put it all back so I winked at my Troop Corporal and he turned away and disappeared. The next moment there was a staccato burst of Besa machine-gun fire and I turned to the NAAFI bloke and said, "My God! Those bloody Jerry armoured cars, or tanks, are right up already - you'd better get the hell out of here, and damn quick too, unless you want to be put in the bag."

At that he jumped quickly into his truck without another word and shot off like a bat out of hell. We carried on 'looting.'

Very confused days from then onwards, still doing this rearguard work, and dashing about all over the place, so only scrappy, short diary entries:

'June 24th: All night move once more - very tired.

June 25th: On watch all day - one flap move - nothing much happened except for some shelling.

June 26th: As above - nothing much except usual flaps.

June 27th: Not so bloody quiet - scrap 17 with two very close ones - too bloody close for my liking. Told that Mersa Matruh had fallen again - hells bells!

June 28th: Flap once more - stayed up all blasted night but nothing seen or happened - thank God!'

I was then ordered to go back, with Reggie, to a Tank Delivery Area to pick up as many Valentines and crews that I could and my diary entry for the 30th just shows 'ALEX!!!' and I seem to remember dashing into Alex for a few blessed hours and going into the Beau Rivage Hotel, which we both knew so well, and having some simply wonderful ice-cold beers and sheer bliss! a piping hot bath! The proprietress, a Mrs. Stephenson I believe, was in a high old state of panic and was wondering what on earth was going to happen - but Reggie and I tried to calm her down saying that we had stopped the Jerries a day or so earlier and that everything would be alright. I picked up just seven Valentines and crews on July 4th, rejoining the Regiment the next day. My diary entries for the next few days merely stated 'just sat about on watch - nothing much happening - casual shelling and odd movements on horizon, etc.' I think that the situation was that the Jerries were every bit as exhausted as we were after the last hectic weeks and were reaching the end of their lines of communication. It also indicated that they were regrouping for yet another thrust.

We had by then moved into a position around about a place called El Alamein which was a nondescript station just below a small, low escarpment overlooking the main track and narrow road leading up to The Wire. On July 8th we were told - at last - we were to be pulled out for a complete rest - marvellous news. My diary entry, however, for July 9th says, 'Relief - bloody hell! We've moved back again into the Alamein Box to prepare for an imminent German attack...' Once again we were a completely scratch force of about eight or nine tanks commanded by Major Bob Lindsay, who won a DSO and MC with us and then went on to command the 44th RTR. The position we were

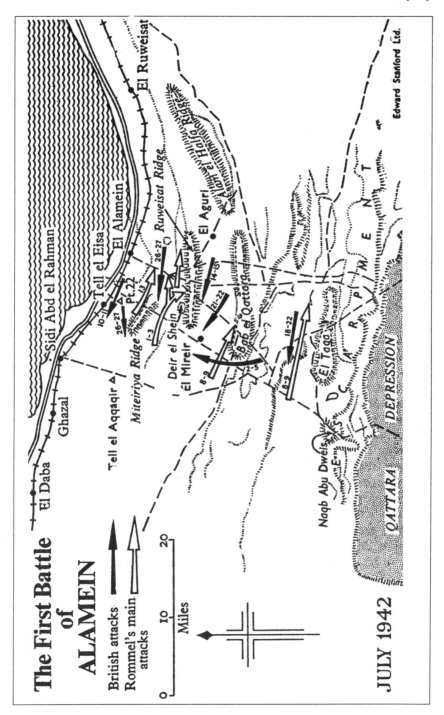

The First Battle of ALAMEIN

British attacks
Rommel's main attacks

Miles

JULY 1942

Edward Stanford Ltd.

holding was a small escarpment overlooking the main road from Alexandria to Mersa Matruh - and then on to Tobruk. Behind us in a small depression were a few 25-pdrs and allegedly in and around us were meant to be some infantry but we never ever saw them. We were thus a very small force - very depleted and utterly exhausted.

Bob had to go off for briefing orders that evening and it was late when he returned, looking very serious, and he ordered all tank commanders and crews to report to him. He explained that the situation was extremely bad: that we were pretty well the last line of defence and that we had instructions, at all costs, to hold our ground and that there would be no retreat whatsoever.

There was almost a sense of relief when he said that last remark because we had been on the run back for so long. Now at last, thank God! here we were to stop and stand. He went on to say that a German attack was expected at dawn the next day and, as a result, we had to be particularly alert for this so the officers, i.e. he and the two Troop Leaders would take the dawn watch. It was imperative to be awake and alert for this.

I went back to my scratch Troop - Sgt. Simpkins MM was acting Troop Sergeant - I can't remember what had happened to Tilford MM - I think that his tank must have been knocked out sometime earlier. I said, "You all heard what Major Lindsay had to say so we have all got to be extremely careful and nobody - and I mean nobody - will fall asleep on sentry duty and everyone will make absolutely sure that the person they relieve is fully awake and able to take over." I then turned to Sgt. Simpkins and said, "You will do duty the hour before me and then you come and wake me up." I then went to the side of my tank and crashed out asleep. As I have mentioned before, we were all completely and utterly exhausted, both physically and mentally, because we had been in continuous action for something like five weeks and we were just like walking automatons.

You know that marvellous feeling you have, just before you wake up in the morning, when you are semi-conscious, and you sort of stretch luxuriously - well, I remember doing that and feeling the heat of the rising sun on my face and I could hear someone whistling and there was the marvellous smell of bacon being cooked when I suddenly sat bolt upright and thought, "God Almighty! I never went on sentry duty! That bloody man Simpkins fell asleep and he never woke me up!"

I jumped up out of my blankets and ran across to his tank and he was just huddled underneath his blankets and I tore them off him and savagely shook him and I think I even kicked him as well, exclaiming, "What the hell was the matter with you! You fell asleep you bloody man! You never woke me up and I'll have your stripes off you for this." He was an awful looking sight, he was unshaven, dirty with red-rimmed eyes and both his hands were bandaged with desert sores. He looked up at me blearily and then rather angrily said, "I bloody well woke you Sir." "No you didn't" I said. "Yes I did!" he said, "I woke you up twice." I said, "What!"

He then went on to explain that he had come over and woken me up the first time and I was extremely angry and rude and swore like hell at him and I then irritably said, "Oh! Alright" and he walked away and then turned round and saw that I had gone flat on my back again. So he came and woke me a second time. I was not quite so angry and I didn't swear at him this time and I said, "OK I'm alright, off you go." So he walked back to his tank but just before he got into his blankets he looked over at me again and saw me sitting up and putting on one of my desert boots. He thought that was alright and just crashed off to sleep.

I remembered then, when he told me that, that when I woke up I had found one of my legs was outside the blankets with my boot on and it was obvious to me that I had fallen back once more and had gone off to sleep a third time so I had never gone on sentry duty at all.

If there had been a German breakthrough at that point and if I had survived and there had been, eventually, a court martial to find out how and why that had happened without any warning or information coming from me - well I wouldn't have had a leg to stand on.

How on earth could I have possibly expected, several weeks later, for anyone on the court who was fresh from a good night's sleep, bathed, shaved, in clean, fresh clothes, to understand that I was completely at the end of my tether, that I was not compos mentis and that I was simply and utterly exhausted both physically and mentally - as indeed we all were. Most certainly I would have been for the high jump.

We stayed up there for the next two or three days and it wasn't particularly pleasant because the 25-pounders behind us were blasting away all the time, right over the tops of our heads, and the noise was deafening. The blasted Stukas came over seven or eight times each day as well, trying to blast the hell out of the guns and us and in one particular raid I was caught out in the open and just had time to dive under the nearest tank with another tank crew man. He was huddled right next to me and got badly hit in the leg with a bomb splinter but I was unhurt.

Two rather odd things happened up here during this short period. One morning, towards mid-day, a lone Italian M.13 Tank came waddling down the main road just below us and everyone opened up like mad, but the shooting was pretty poor and it took a hell of a lot of shots before it was hit and stopped and white flags appeared out of the top of the turret and the wretched crew scrambled out and surrendered to us. Just what it was doing on its own goodness only knows. The other incident was also rather strange.

The next day I suddenly spotted, with my binoculars, about ten German Panzer Mark III's moving in a tight 'V' formation parallel to us but unfortunately out of range, so I reported this back to Brigade on the radio. The Brigadier himself got on the air and asked me to go on reporting their movements so I gave a running commentary on what they were doing. I reported that it was almost as if they were on manoeuvres on a parade ground as they kept in immaculate formation, first of all broadside on and then they all wheeled left and came up towards us and then, damn it, they wheeled left again and went back the way they had come, all the time without firing a shot and all of them completely closed down. Unfortunately, again, they were still out of range.

However, down across the road from us and well concealed, was a portee, this being a 2-pdr gun mounted on a lorry chassis and much closer to them. The gunner carefully waited until the leading tanks had gone past him and then, with splendid shooting, he picked off two of the rear tanks and the others just carried on without taking any action. It was most extraordinary to watch and the Brigadier was highly delighted with the result.

We then moved up - a day or so after the above incidents - to help support some Australian infantry who were going in to do a dawn attack with us around Tel-el-Eisa, and on the move up as we were fairly near the coast we had to drive across a salt pan and the blinding sun reflected cruelly on the eyes from the white crystals of salt and sand. Two or three lorries had got themselves well and truly bogged down and, inevitably, with the volume of traffic trying to go round them left and right other vehicles started to get bogged down also, breaking up the hard crust, and tanks were called in to try and pull

them out, and even some of the tanks got bogged down, including my
own, the left track sinking down so the tank was angled up with the
right hand side pointing up in the air. I was idly sitting on the turret
smoking and quite enjoying my forced inactivity when I heard the
drone of an aircraft and saw a lone Macchi-Fiat CR42 fighter coming
from our lines, i.e. going due west. It was obviously in trouble because
it was going very slowly and very low, only about 800-900 feet up and
it was trailing a thin spume of glycol, a sort of white misty vapour
behind it, I yelled to my driver to start up the engine so that I could
have power for the traverse, switched the Besa machine-gun to high
rate of fire (1200 rounds per minute) and waited, and as he came
overhead I very carefully aimed-off and put pretty well the full belt of
240 rounds into it. I could see the tracer absolutely eating into the
fuselage. It carried on for a few more moments and then the thin grey
spume changed to thick black smoke and it went into a shallow dive
and disappeared out of sight over the crest of a very small ridge. There
was an almighty whumph and clouds of black smoke and the chaps all
around me exclaimed excitedly, "You got it Sir! You got the bloody
thing, well done!"

Whether or not I actually shot it down I'm not certain but I'm pretty
sure I hastened its demise. Anyway I proudly claimed to having shot
down an Italian Fighter plane! It was a biplane similar to our Gloster
Gladiator. I was proud to have a 'kill' because I was after the plane and
not the pilot and I'm afraid that I didn't think very much about the
poor unfortunate man.

Later, when we had just had our usual 'O' Group Orders for the
forthcoming attack, done in the traditional format and style of: 1.
Information; 2. Intention; 3. Method; 4. Plan; 5. Administration; 6.
Questions etc. I then noticed a crowd of Aussie infantry gathering
around an empty 44-gallon oil-drum to get their orders, so I wandered
up to hear how this was to be done.

They were an incredibly scruffy crowd with no one appearing to be
dressed the same: some stripped to the waist with dirty, ragged shorts
and scuffed boots: others in dirty slacks and equally dirty singlets:
some wearing slouch hats, others with tin hats or bare-headed: talking,
smoking and laughing amongst themselves as they grouped around
this oil-drum and waited for an RSM to stand on the top of it.

He looked magnificent and would have done credit to a Guards
battalion. He was a good 6' tall with a fine physique to match: deeply

bronzed and bare chested: wearing immaculately clean and well-pressed shorts, puttees and highly polished boots and a clean slouch hat with polished chin strap.

He stood with his hands on his hips, looking down at them and bellowed, "Friends, Romans and Countrymen" - this is going to be good I thought - "lend me yer fuckin' ears you heap! You lucky bastards are going to have the chance once more of putting the shits up the fuckin' Jerries! Aren't you the lucky ones...!"

Modesty prevents me from printing the oaths and obscenities which greeted his remarks but if Aussie discipline was very much their own then so was their courage and fighting ability.

The dawn sortie with the Aussies was successful and they got established at Tel-el-Eisa with comparatively few casualties, also ourselves, as the Jerries were also quite exhausted and in not very great strength up there. The great day finally arrived and at long last we were relieved and pulled right out and went back to Sidi Bishr.

El Alamein

The next few weeks of complete rest, relaxation and leave worked absolute wonders for all of us and we very quickly recovered as a result of being free of the frights, flaps and alarms we had been experiencing over the past many months.

Many new faces were around as we had been reinforced because of our losses and I was particularly pleased to see amongst the batch of new officers a friend of mine, John Herbertson, whom I'd met previously in England before we came overseas. He eventually became a captain in a TA Regiment and was so fed up with being stuck in the UK that he volunteered to drop a pip and he came out to us as a lieutenant. He joined 'A' Squadron, later became the Adjutant and eventually my second in command in 'B' Squadron in Italy, earning a well-deserved MBE.

We knew that something big was brewing up once more owing to the various buzzes going around and the obvious influx of troops, equipment etc. and we were all wondering what part we were going to have to play in it.

I was feeling particularly pleased at that time because it was hinted that we were going to get the new Sherman tank which had just arrived and this had a 75 millimetre gun firing a 15 pound shell and we thought at long last we would be on equal terms with the Jerries; also my third pip and gong had come through so life seemed pretty good.

Imagine our great disappointment, then, when we were informed that we were not going to get the new Sherman tank but that we were to be re-equipped, once again, with blasted Valentines with their pathetic little 2-pdr pop-gun, and that we would be joining the 23rd Armoured Brigade. This was a new Brigade just out from England consisting of the 40th, 46th and 50th RTR - territorial battalions. It was reckoned that the forthcoming battle was going to be a very tough one indeed and that they should have the backing of a battle experienced Valentine Tank Regiment - and that was why we were joining them.

However we were promised, definitely this time, that as soon as a breakthrough had been achieved then our job would have been done and we would then be very definitely pulled out for a complete rest - a long one - and a complete refit, but as we had heard that so many times before we all took it with a very large pinch of salt. The BBC back at home on the 28th September 1942 had broadcast a record of the Regiment's activities in the Western Desert which I quote:

BBC News Excerpt - 28/9/42

The 8th Battalion of the Royal Tank Regiment has just completed a year's unbroken war service in the Western Desert and here are some of the things it has done. In November it advanced with the New Zealand Division: marched on Benghazi and Aggedabia with the Fourth Indian Division: withdrew to the Gazala Line with the First Armoured Division and then went "on column" with the 50th Division and the Guards Brigade. It has been loaned out so many times that an officer of the Battalion remarks, "We fight for who feeds us."

At the end of May the Battalion fought an action against 70 German Mark III and Mark IV tanks supported by artillery and the odds were two to one against. Within the next two to three days it attacked and routed an enemy column and assisted two of our Brigades who were being attacked by 60 Mark III's and IV's and many 88-millimetre anti-tank guns.

On June 2nd it fought perhaps its most successful action. Armoured cars had discovered that the enemy were laying an ambush against one of our columns. The 8th Battalion and supporting artillery went into action and forced the enemy to withdraw.

A few days later it covered the evacuation of the Guards Brigade from the Knightsbridge area, fighting the rearguard action alone for 2½ hours. For an hour and half of that time the enemy were within 400 yards of the Battalion's leaguer and yet the 8th Battalion pulled out of the very critical position at the appointed time.

The Battalion was one of the units covering the withdrawal into Tobruk and again took the rearguard, remaining at the gap in the minefield until dawn. The men were so tired that some slept standing up in their tanks. The next day 11 of its tanks took part in the brilliant extraction of the 50th Division through the Italian lines. On the march the fuel lorry was hit and to make the supplies last out the tanks had to be driven in pairs, one towing another. Five of the nine survivors were fighting at Capuzzo the day after.

The withdrawal to Alamein was the most arduous journey the Battalion ever made and upon its arrival it went into action to help halt the German advance. From the Alamein Box it joined the Australians in their sortie westwards.

Its Regimental Records also include this story from an attack in the Cauldron Area. One of the Battalion's tanks was hit and stopped. The radio was still working and these were the messages sent by the Officer in command of it. "My tank has been hit and won't move. The 2-pounder is bent too but the 'Besa' is still working. I can work the 'Besa' myself so I am sending the crew back. I am being hit quite a lot now and the enemy is closing in fast... they are about 400 yards away now... the gun crews don't like being 'Besa'd'... I've been hit again and the tank is on fire... it's getting too hot in here now so I'll smash the wireless and try to get out... There are a hell of a lot of Bosche all around my tank. Well here goes. Cheerio!"

The 8th Battalion was withdrawn on July 17th.

This time the 23rd Armoured Brigade was to be in 30 Corps and we were to be attached to the 1st South African Division. We therefore left 'the flesh pots' and moved back up into 'the blue' once more and started to liaise furiously for the forthcoming battle. The main road and railway line from Alexandria up to Mersa Matruh were running parallel to the sea, the railway about two miles away from it, and El Alamein was merely a small station on this railway near a small hill on part of the escarpment. The front line ran just in front of Alamein for about 30 miles due south down to Himeimat which was on the edge of the Quattara Depression. This depression was a huge one full of soft sand and it was quite impossible going for vehicles - so the front line was firmly anchored from the sea in the north to this soft sand in the south.

This is where the 8th Army in its headlong retreat back in July had stopped and dug itself in and by now the line was very, very strong indeed with thousands, if not hundreds of thousands, of mines being sown, barbed wire, dug-in infantry and gun positions, dug-in tanks and reserves all over the place. It was really rather like a World War One situation with a short front which was very strongly held. The Germans and Italians were doing the same sort of thing and ultimately, just before the battle started, there must have been anything up to half a million troops, with all their equipment, facing one another for a real dog-fight.

The Powers-that-be occasionally had bright ideas and as most units up in the desert by then were pretty well trained, or had been training very hard, some bright boy up at Army Headquarters thought out the splendid idea that each unit should send parties for a 48-hour break right down on the coast - which was only about eight to ten miles away in our case - so that they could relax completely with nothing to do. No guard duties, no fatigues, nothing whatsoever. They could bathe, sun-bathe, they could sleep, they could do exactly what they liked. It was a marvellous idea and every unit in the area did this.

We, the 8th RTR, had our own small camp which was situated in the sand dunes and it really was great fun to relax completely like this just swimming, sun-bathing and doing nothing.

Nobody, of course, had any swimming trunks and I suppose there were the best part of up to 1,000 bodies up and down the beach in weird and wonderful suntanned colours. Some people, like myself, were deeply bronzed down to the waist and then a white area where we had been wearing shorts and then bronzed legs. Others were multi-coloured having kept their shirts and stockings on so that their faces and forearms and knees were brown, in patches, whilst others were fairly new to the desert and looked rather white.

I had had a swim and was drying myself when I heard a chap excitedly shouting out, "Hem, Hem" (not 'Ham'). He was a South African called Bunny Rightford and I had known him in 1938 when he was a lance-corporal in the 5th RTR. He had very rapidly been promoted to sergeant, had won a Military Medal and had recently been commissioned and was now a lieutenant with the South African Armoured Division. Apparently he was attached to one of the brand new tank regiments in the 23rd Armoured Brigade, who were with us, and quite how he recognised me out of the 1000-odd naked bodies, well I'll leave that to your imagination!

He said that these chaps were completely new to the desert and they hadn't got a clue how to live in it. They were living pretty starkly and pretty roughly because they had no Officers' mess of any description: were sleeping beside their tanks: they didn't augment their rations so they were existing on the ordinary day-to-day rations and he was complaining bitterly about this.

I was the Squadron PMC (President Messing Committee) so I had taken all the Squadron Officers' pay books from them, collected their money, doled out a few quid to each and gave the rest to the Squadron Mess Corporal and had given him orders to go back into Alexandria and buy all the possible goodies that he could, i.e. beer, hooch, food, cigars etc. because we were living on the basis of "eat, drink, and be merry because tomorrow we die."

I invited him over to our Mess for dinner that evening and the Mess once again consisted of the top of a 3-ton lorry on the ground. He came over and we had beer, sherry and gin before the meal; we had wine with it and it consisted of fresh asparagus, soup, eggs on steak, fruit salad augmented with fresh oranges and apples, followed by coffee, port, brandy and cigars.

Bunny was absolutely ecstatic at having such a superb meal and he got completely and utterly plastered, in fact he was paralytic, and we literally had to carry him back to his truck and he was swearing eternal friendship and saying what fucking marvellous blokes we were and what a fucking way to live and that was the last I saw or heard of him. I sincerely hope he survived the war because he really was a great character.

I said there were a lot of new faces and we had a new CO of whom we weren't quite sure because he didn't seem to be a fighting soldier, rather more an administrative type bloke. He called me into his tent one day, 21st October, and said, "Ham I have got some news for you which you won't like but it's an order so you will just have to listen and take it." He then went on to say that the forthcoming battle was going to be a very tough one indeed as a result of which heavy casualties were expected and as I was the senior Captain in the Regiment and probably one of the most experienced tank commanders, being one of the old originals left, that I was going to be "LOB" (Left Out of Battle). I was absolutely furious but he said it was no good being furious about it as this was being done to all Regiments. "You are going back to a holding tank unit so that as and when we get casualties you will come up and take over and knowing how you feel about your old Troop it has been decided that in your Squadron your complete Troop

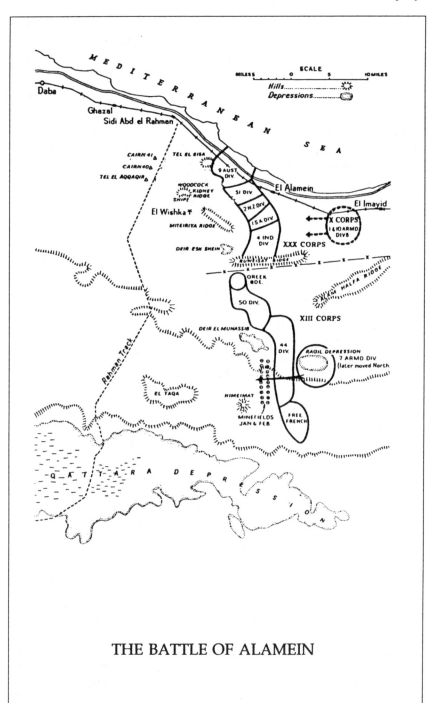

THE BATTLE OF ALAMEIN

is going back with you," and he said there would be quite a large nucleus of chaps waiting to come up again as and when called for.

I could see the sense and reasoning for this but I was very upset and extremely downcast when I said goodbye to the Squadron and my fellow officers when I left on the 21st to go back to Sidi Bishr. History shows that the battle for Alamein started at 21.40 hours on the night of October 23rd when something like 1000 guns opened up an artillery barrage - the heaviest concentration of guns and gunfire since World War One.

Although I was something like 35 miles back at base camp, even at that distance we could hear the continuous rumble of this terrific barrage and the sky to the west was aglow with the reflected gun flashes and I remember thinking at the time, "Thank God I'm not at the receiving end of that lot."

The next day, as the balloon had gone up I asked the Camp Commandant if it was OK to pass the information that I had to the rest of my chaps and he agreed with this. So I assembled all the 8th RTR and gave them a short lecture on what was happening and how the battle was going to be carried out. Apparently this went down very well and they started to pass the gen on to other chaps in the camp who approached me and asked would I give the lecture a second time and so with the Camp Commandant's permission I did this once more.

It was an extremely anxious and fretful time being back at base camp and knowing what was going on and that we were not there, and all sorts of buzzes and rumours were flying around but we just had to sit back and wait.

To my relief on October 31st the Camp Commandant called me in and handed me a message, saying "I expect this is what you have been waiting for." It was a request for so many NCOs, drivers, gunners, ie tank crews, to be despatched immediately back up to the 8th RTR and it did stress one officer was required. So I said to the Camp Commandant: "Right, that's me, I'll take the detachment off," and back we went up to join the 8th and actually reached them on the evening of November lst.

The journey up the rear areas was really rather awe inspiring as the amount of stuff on the ground was absolutely incredible. It was extremely well organised but the closer we got to the sharp end the more and more chaotic and confused it seemed to become. With the passage of so many thousands of vehicles the desert sand had been absolutely ground into a fine powdered dust and there was dust absolutely everywhere. The setting sun was pretty nearly obscured by this, and of course the dust being kicked up by the constant firing of guns and the frequent bombings by the Luftwaffe trying to hit the gun positions and our lines of supply and communications. I stopped somewhere near our rendezvous and got out of my truck to speak to four New Zealand Bofors ack-ack gunners and whilst talking to them and asking for directions for the particular track I needed there was a sudden scream and whistle as six or more shells landed all around us.

We were completely enveloped in dust and sand and when it all cleared the four Kiwis were lying on top of each other in a slit trench but I was still standing with my hands in my pockets and my pipe in my mouth. They got up and started to dust themselves down and wanted to know what the fucking hell I thought I was doing and that I wasn't going to be standing around for fucking long if I was going to do that stupid sort of fucking thing!

What they didn't know was that when the shells landed, as it happened all so very quickly, that I clenched my fists so tightly in my pockets that I broke the linings of my shorts so that my fists were stuck tight and I just couldn't get my ruddy pipe out of my mouth! Nonchalance somewhat misunderstood!

As I walked away I suddenly burst into laughter and they must have thought that I was quite mad as I couldn't help remembering the Kiwi infantryman I had picked-up at Sidi Rezegh in '41 when he went storming off into the night swearing his head off and saying he was going to fuck off for ever from the fucking war.

The first person I met on rejoining the 8th RTR was Berry Veale who was then our second in command, and I was astonished, to put it mildly, at his reaction on seeing me. I thought there would be a pleasant smile and a handshake but not a bit of it. He was absolutely livid and wanted to know what the hell I was doing up there, I had no right to be there at all etc. etc. When I protested and said I had been ordered to bring up a detachment he asked, "Where is that order?" and of course I couldn't produce it and he got hopping mad and said he would make damn sure that I would go straight back at first light. I was most puzzled by this as he walked away and I can only assume with hindsight that the 8th had already gone through a very nasty sticky period up at Alamein and that this combined with the strain and stress we had been through over the rest of the year must have made him somewhat edgy because I had never seen him like that before.

I reported to our new CO, 'Bam' and I was surprised and rather dismayed to find him at the very back of his tank on his knees eating a meal and wearing a steel helmet - I had never ever seen anybody in the 8th wear a steel helmet before. He said he was pleased to see me and I had better go across to 'B' Squadron. This I did and I was even more dismayed to see that Charles 'Batty' Attwood, who was then commanding the Squadron because George had been wounded and gone back to England, was also wearing a tin hat. When I ticked him off about this, he looked at me rather sheepishly and said, "Well things are a bit hot up here old boy and there is all sorts of stuff flying about all the time." I then met good old Sergeant Simpkins MM who came up to me and said, "Thank Christ you're back here again sir, things are very dodgy and they are not the same."

George Sutton had been wounded and gone back to England. Reggie Campbell had been promoted and gone to 'C' Squadron and as I was "Left Out Of Battle" there were only two subalterns who had had fighting experience, Mike and Leo, and there were three brand new ones. Also, with the casualties in tank crews there were many replacements around and I felt rather disturbed about all this.

The 8th were going in that evening on a night attack and I asked if I could join in but I was emphatically told "no" and that I was to stay out of it completely.

In they went and had an extremely tough and very bitter battle in support of units of the 51st Highland Division and that night out of 34 tanks, all we could muster out of 52, the 8th lost another 22 tanks.

The 8th had had a pretty heavy bashing by then, in fact very heavy indeed, and the next day, November 4th, I took over a Troop once more in a very composite bunch attack moving up to the old position at Tel-el-Eisa (The Hill of Jesus). This was where, on the run back from Gazala in July earlier that year, Major Bob Lindsay had told us, "No more retreating - this is where we stand and stay."

Nothing much seemed to happen that day except more intermittent shelling and bombing and then the news came through, on November 5th, that the breakthrough had been achieved and that the Axis forces were in full retreat. This was terrific and to our amazement the 'Powers-that-be' remembered their promise to us and ordered us to pull out and hand over our remaining tanks to the 50th RTR. This we did and then got onto lorries and hightailed right back to Alex for a long rest and complete refit.

As I did not take part in any of the actual battles at El Alamein, apart from the above-mentioned skirmish, I am not therefore in a position to comment about it or give any personal views but I would like to mention Major Brian F. McCabe, MC and Bar, who was the 'A' Squadron Commander there. He did a magnificent job though I think he lost the entire Squadron and his wounds were so severe that he had to go back to England for pretty well the rest of the war. A superb book that gives the overall picture of the battle is *Alamein* by C.E. Lucas Phillips, a most splendid book. Another detailed one, showing all units of the RTR taking part, is Volume II of *The Tanks* by Captain Liddell Hart.

*   *   *

The 8th Tanks were very lucky indeed with the quality of the men who served with them, as I think the two following stories will illustrate.

Lieutenant Bill Fairclough MC was with 'A' Squadron and at Alamein, when he bailed out of the third tank which had been shot from under him in three successive days, he was so angry that he walked towards the German positions and stood in front of them and shouted out what bloody rotten shots they were - that three times they had tried to get him and missed - he didn't care a bugger what they were going to do in the future. He lit a cigarette, gave them a 'V for Victory' signal and just turned round and calmly walked back. Unfortunately, but I suppose inevitably with a man of that character, he pushed his luck too hard and was killed a few days later.

The other story concerns Lieutenant Michael Hunt who was in 'B' Squadron. Again, whilst at Alamein, Mike did an incredibly brave thing. The Squadron was supporting some infantry in a very murderous attack and Mike stopped his tank at point-blank range and got out and picked-up four or five badly wounded infantry men and lifted them onto the back of his tank - all the time under intensive fire. He ordered his driver to pull out and, owing to the heavy enemy fire, he laid across them so that his body would give them some sort of protection. Unfortunately a shell landed on the back of the tank blowing them all off, so Mike calmly stopped the tank and lifted them all back again - once again pulling out under heavy enemy fire.

Cruelly, the shell landing on the back further injured the already wounded men, one being killed at the time, and two of the others died of their wounds later. Incredibly, Mike himself was unhurt and he was most deservedly recommended for a Victoria Cross for this very fine and very brave act. However, most tragically, he was killed a day or so later and to the utter disgust of his parents he was merely awarded a posthumous Mention in Despatches.

I understand that the reason that he did not receive a VC was that there had to be a least two independent witnesses for an act to be worthy of the award of a VC and that, in this case, they were either killed at the time or died later before being able to verify and confirm this splendid and most courageous action of Michael Hunt.

He was a splendid Officer, a fine man and super bloke and was most popular and liked by everyone. He was very greatly missed and I am proud to have known him and to have had him as a friend.

This ends the sojourn of the 8th Battalion of the Royal Tank Regiment in the Western Desert from August 1941 to November 1942.

In October 1992 I went to Egypt to attend the ceremony commemorating the 50th Anniversary of the Battle of El Alamein and found Mike's name inscribed in the Remembrance Book at the Commonwealth Cemetery there. Unfortunately I was unable to find his grave, which is one of 7367 buried there - with a further 11,945 honoured on the walls of the lovely Cloisters. He was very much in my thoughts however at that time and place as were so many other fine men of the Regiment.

*   *   *

I have been asked several times, since the end of the war, whether or not I was ever frightened and my answer to that is rather curious as my reply has been 'no' and 'yes.' The reason for this odd reply is that I believe that one went through various stages, with each stage getting progressively worse the longer one was up the sharp end.

Phase I: Battle Initiation

Once one went through the first shock of battle and survived it, then this was OK.

Phase II: Battle Hardened

This was a good stage as one had become experienced and knew what it was like and what to expect. One could trust one's crew, Squadron, equipment, etc. and, above all else, one's self. There was almost a sense of exhilaration and even excitement during this period and this lasted, for me at any rate, through much of the Desert fighting. However, by the time we had got back to Alamein in July 1942 after five or six weeks of very hard, bitter fighting I was certainly beginning to move onto Phase III.

Phase III: Battle Weary

By now a little of the 'gung-ho' attitude had given way to a more cautious one - thinking a bit more of the possible consequences of being hit and hurt and the excitement had been considerably dulled by then. In fact things were beginning to get just a little grim. In Italy in 1944, after being out of action for just about a year, I started off in Phase II but quickly moved on to Phase III owing to the very heavy sustained shelling, mortaring and 'stonking' we then experienced. The extremely difficult and totally different terrain after the wide and open desert, where at least we could move about if things got too hot, made this action impossible and we just had to sit and take it. Not at all funny. Casualties too were heavier and in a much shorter space of time. Things were decidedly grim by now.

Phase IV: Battle Weary

This was very definitely the worst stage of the lot and I was beginning to wonder just how much more I could take. Phase III was bad enough but now one was beginning to think, and say, on being told we were on operations once more, "Christ! Not us again! Not my Squadron! Not me! Isn't some other bastard fighting this bloody war?" etc. I had seen so many good friends and good men 'get the chop' by then that I felt my number must be coming up soon... As one of the very few 'old desert hands' left I was expected, automatically, to show coolness, confidence and a complete disregard to anything 'unpleasant' and this was a very heavy responsibility under these conditions.

In the Desert, then, I do not recall being, what I would say, really frightened - scared yes - but in Italy, well I was bloody terrified.

2
Palestine, Syria, Egypt 1943-1944

This was an extremely unhappy period for us and it is rather interesting that I cannot find any diaries for 1943. So these notes are bound to be rather scrappy as they rely entirely upon memory. On November 10th 1942 we arrived at Raffa in Palestine. It was miles from anywhere and there was nothing to distinguish it from anything else and the men christened it The Arsehole of the World; so that gives you a pretty good idea of what it was like. Apparently on the 14th I managed to get into Jerusalem and on the 20th we celebrated, in great style, Cambrai Day. It is a big event in the Royal Tank Regiment's history.

On November 27th we had a visit from the new Commander-in-Chief, General Alexander and he seemed a fine chap and created a certain amount of consternation and alarm, to our great delight, for our CO who had made us practice, for two or three days, marching and saluting and all that rigmarole, and everything was blancoed and whitewashed. When he asked Alex if he would like to see the Regiment march pass, after Alex had spoken individually to all the officers, Alex said, "Good heavens no! I want to have a look at the cook house," and in horror the CO turned round and in a squeaky voice shouted for the Quarter Master and off they went - it's probably the one place they never expected the Commander-in-Chief to visit.

On December 7th an absolute tragedy occurred. We had hired six remount horses from a cavalry depot nearby for anybody who wanted to take up horse riding. One of the 'C' Squadron officers, Peter Kitto - the young officer I had picked up in my taxi service in the run back to Tobruk just before Tobruk fell - had been wounded three times and he had just come back and he went out that morning to do some riding. On coming back to camp the horse bolted and rushed straight back to where the stables were, which consisted of bare concrete underground shelters underneath a building, and it slipped on the concrete and rolled heavily and threw Peter against a concrete pillar and crushed him and unfortunately he died from his injuries the next day. It was a damn shame, he was a fine chap and had been wounded three times and to go this way, well, was just so unfair. He was very popular and was sadly missed by all of us.

On 21st December there was a special memorial service in the Church of Nativity at Bethlehem for all members of the 8th who had died in the desert campaign, which was very moving.

Quite naturally the long rest and relaxation, the endless swimming - because we were right on the coast - and plenty of sport - hockey, football, rugger etc. soon got us back to being very fit both physically and mentally, but inevitably one started to get tired and bored with this, even with the endless opportunities of leave and going to see all the rather magnificent places in this part of the world that one had read about in the Bible.

I managed to get into Damascus on two or three different occasions and what a fascinating old city it was. I went down into the souk and delighted in watching the skill of the Arabs as they made, and inscribed, so delicately, beautiful silver-work and their skills must have been handed down over generations.

Similarly, watching the superb designs and patterns they weaved on their beautiful and famous Damascan brocades and rugs was another delight. In their Arab robes and with their wrinkled, gnarled, brown faces - well - it took one back into Biblical times. I did buy some brocade and silverware for my wife but unfortunately she never received them. Either they were stolen or sunk in transit.

Beirut was another superb city with marvellous buildings, views and wonderful food at The Lucullus restaurant. Sitting there on the balcony, overlooking the lovely blue Mediterranean sea, drinking wine with a splendid meal was simply incredible and a far cry from the hellish time we had been going through when fighting so hard and desperately during Rommel's push in May/June/July during the Khamsin season.

(What a complete tragedy now, the way this lovely city has been torn apart and destroyed in the most stupid of civil wars).

A trip to the famous Ruins of Baalbeck - believed to be one of the eight wonders of the world - was another unforgettable experience. Photographs do not do justice to this remarkable place. The ruins of the Temple of Jupiter were said to be some 2,300 years old; had taken 250 years to build: the columns were 100 feet high and seven feet in circumference and 150 tons in weight.

The Temple of Bacchus was capable of holding up to 30,000 people and the mind simply boggled at the thought of the tremendous achievement in building these places and at what horrendous cost of

1. 8th RTR Battle Flag. In fact a German ground-to-air recognition flag - scarlet with black swastika on white background - captured at Bardia 31st December 1941. The Germans would place this in front of their positions so that they would not be bombed by the Luftwaffe, as recognition was very difficult in the desert (we were bombed by the Desert Air Force on one occasion and twice we saw, to our great delight, Stuka dive bombers hit their own troops).

The five columns to the right of the swastika are the names of the officers who served with the 8th RTR. The first column and the first eight names in the second column are the 'originals' who left England in April 1941.

The two columns on the left of the swastika are the battle honours won in the Desert and in Italy.

The flag is now in the Tank Museum at Bovington.

2. Fort Capuzzo, November 1941. 'B' Squadron's first battle (with the New Zealand Division).

3. Sidi Rezegh 1941. Knocked-out in my first tank battle. My gunner unfortunately killed.

4. Sidi Rezegh Tomb, November 1941. Very heavy fighting here. Note German graves in foreground.

5. Sidi Rezegh, November 1941. "Three left out of 13" after the first week of the six-and-a-half week campaign: L-R, Reggie Campbell MC (wounded and burnt); Hickey Sugden MC & bar (twice wounded); Self ("a slight scratch"). Background: Tony Reid, Recce Officer, killed at Bardia, December 1941.

6. German Panzer Mark III. Knocked-out in Sidi Rezegh area. A good tank with a 50mm gun and two MGs, with a five man crew.

7. Tobruk outskirts, 1941. Handing over our Valentines - just seven left out of 52. Note hit on turret of leading tank. Mine is fifth or sixth, still with holes in turret.

9. Bardia, December 1941. Turret of Matilda tank captured and concreted into ground and used as an armoured pill-box. About 4 inches of armour: very difficult to knock out.

8. 'C' Squadron, November/December 1941. L-R, Hickey Sugden MC & bar; Peter Kitto; Tony Reid; Bertie Keelan; Ian Taylor. Peter, Tony and Ian killed: Bertie wounded.

10. Our tanks before Bardia attack: bunched-up for propaganda photograph. The white-red-white identification stripes were soon covered with oil and sand as they proved too easy an aiming point for the Germans.

11, 12 & 13. German 88mm knocked out by Hickey Sugden, who stalked it after it had killed his friend Tony Reid. Note 2-pdr shell holes in gun shield. Hickey Sugden and Tony Reid.

14. 'B' Squadron, January/February 1942, Benghazi area. L-R, Reggie Campbell; Mike Hunt; Peter Butt; Leo Stock; self. Mike, Peter and Leo killed. Mike recommended for a posthumous VC at Alamein, but did not get it.

15. My tank en route for Benghazi, early January 1942. Very cold wind hence leather jerkin, gloves etc.

16. "HAM-BROS!" El Adem, February 1942. Self with elder brother Gerald (Captain, RASC), who turned up with a crate of beer.

17. March/April 1942. Douglas Dawson, Charles 'Batty' Attwood, Leslie 'Doc' Milton, George Sutton.

18. Our tanks disguised, using "sunshields," as lorries, whilst on a raid behind enemy lines during the 'Pimple' attack. We are in a rather large 'Deir' - or depression - in the desert.

19. Bliss! Sunset in the desert, April/May 1942.

20. Tamar area May/June 1942. Different types of desert terrain showing thorny scrub and loose sandy pebbles. Tank tracks in foreground. Heavy tank battles here during this period. Vehicles on horizon - "Whose? Theirs or Ours?" "Don't know old boy - you'd better go and have a 'shufti'."

21. Knightsbridge area, May/June 1942. Hard, stony ground littered with small rocks. Hellish going for trucks, particularly ambulances with wounded. Eventually known as The Cauldron, and the scene of heavy fighting, 8th Army losing a big tank battle. Believe it or not the thin black line in the foreground is a Bedouin Arab with his flock of goats.

22. Khamsin sandstorm approaching, June 1942. Could last for two days like this. Absolute misery and heat unbearable.

23. German Panzer Mark IV 'Special' with long-barrelled 75mm firing a 15lb shell. Damn good tank.

24. The Cauldron, June 1942. A quick breather before attacking. Believe they are 4th RTR Valentines. Apparently their white-red-white identification stripes have been erased.

25 & 26. Tank battle casualties. Extricating a wounded map (top) and Military Police extricating a corpse, headless and charred (bottom).

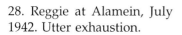

27. Alamein, July 1942. Self; Reggie Campbell; unknown replacement officer killed the next day. Very, very tired. Dessert sores on nose, hands and legs.

28. Reggie at Alamein, July 1942. Utter exhaustion.

29. Alamein, July 1942. Self in centre wearing sun glasses. Pipe in stocking top - never without it! After being told, yet again, that we were being pulled out we were then told to mount a dawn attack the next day - with the Aussies - at Tel El Eisa (the Hill of Jesus).

30. Alamein, October 1942. German Mark IV dug-in near Raham Track.

31. Alamein, October 1942. "The hammering of the Panzers."

32. Bill Fairclough MC. Killed at Alamein October 1942 after being knocked-out of three tanks on three successive days.

33. Doc Leslie Milton. A very popular and well-liked man.

34. Padre Sam Kemble. Equally liked and popular with all in the Regiment.

35. Tel Aviv, Palestine 1943. Self and John Herbertson MBE on leave, my finger fractured playing rugger.

36. My Sherman tank "Hornbill" and crew, Fayid area, Egypt 1944. L-R, Eric Mace (lap gunner); L/Cpl Stanley Shapcott (75mm gunner); L/Cpl Tim Clayton (driver - killed in Gothic Line); 'Curly' Carter (wireless operator - bald as a coot!)

37. Self with "Hornbill."

38. Citta St. Angelo, Italy, May 1944. Captain John Robinson MC and Major Peter Butt receiving two flags from Mayor and ladies who had secretly made them (see text). Now in Tank Museum at Bovington.

39. Croce 1944. Knocked-out Shermans. Bitter fighting here.

40. Monte Gemmano 1944. Heavy machine-gunners firing on the town.

41. Gothic Line 1944. Knocked-out German S/P gun. 155mm?

42. 8th RTR Squadron Commanders, July 1944. L-R, Self; Reggie Campbell MC; Tom Hendrie DSO; Hickey Sugden MC & bar. Self, Reggie and Hickey were the "three originals." Reggie and Tom died after the war.

43. Self just before final battle, April 9th, 1944.

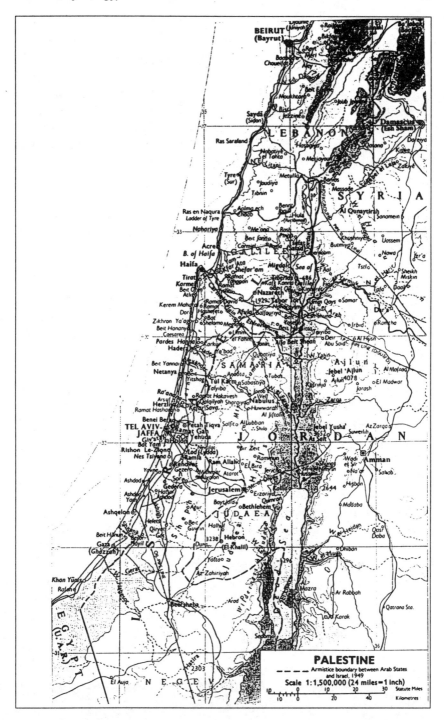

PALESTINE

– – – – Armistice boundary between Arab States
and Israel, 1949

Scale 1:1,500,000 (24 miles=1 inch)

slave labour.

Truly this was a wonderful part of the world to be seeing - at the Army's expense! - and one had a feeling of almost awe and awareness of 'ancient civilisation.'

We had now been abroad for just over two years and were now completely out of the fighting as the 8th Army was victoriously pushing the Axis forces back first out of Libya, then out of Tripolitania and by now they were into Tunisia and we were irked at the thought that we were not participating in this victorious campaign. By now various men were beginning to get unpleasant anonymous letters from home saying that 'they ought to be back and seeing just what their wives were getting up to, etc.' This was most distressing because there was absolutely no hope whatsoever of getting any man back to the UK on compassionate grounds.

My own batman was having this trouble and he came to see if I could do anything possible for him. I couldn't, except write to the local branch of SSAFA where his wife lived which was not of much comfort and help to him at that time. However, I am glad to say that this did eventually resolve itself at the end of the war because I met him again, many years later, at one of the Alamein Reunions I had organised. To my amazement he said to me, rather shyly, in conversation, "We've had a son and I hope you don't mind Sir but we have named him after you." I thought that the Christian names of Joseph Stuart might be a bit of a handicap in the future but I was rather touched by this.

Earlier in the New Year (1943) my Troop Sgt. 'Ticker' Tilford's award of his Military Medal came through - won for his fine effort in May 1942 when Rommel attacked us in the 'Gazala Gallop' battle (my gong was for the same scrap) and naturally we were invited to a celebration in the Sergeants' Mess.

It was some party and eventually he was gently led away, completely plastered, and put to bed in his tent. We returned to their Mess to carry on celebrating. After a little time feeble cries for help were heard so we rushed out to find the silly bugger had a) decided to have a pee or b) to rejoin the party or c) to do both and he had fallen over. Unfortunately, for him, he decided to crawl to the Mess but being totally disorientated he started to crawl the wrong way - into a cactus plantation!

He was taken to hospital and was in there for about ten days as he got blood poisoning from the cactus needles, about 97 being removed from his hands, arms and legs. He was lucky not to be put on a charge for 'self-inflicted injuries!'

We had a very good Rugger XV of which I was a enthusiastic member and I set off one day with most of the team in a lorry for a match. I woke up the next morning in hospital, in a bed in a single ward, not knowing what the hell had happened or where I was. I felt myself but could find nothing broken but when I tried to get up the room swam about and I laid down again.

I pressed a bell but nothing happened and I guessed that we had had a road accident, as I couldn't remember playing, and was worrying about the rest of the team.

The door eventually opened and Doc Leslie Milton came in with a photograph of my wife and I said, "What the hell are you doing with that!" "Thank God! You are conscious you silly sod! You got concussed and knocked-out whilst playing!"

I could remember nothing at all about the game - apparently I was kicked just below my eye and was laid down on the touch-line but I kept getting up and trying to rejoin the game, it didn't matter which side I played for, until I was led away!

In May 1943 Tunis was finally taken and the Germans and Italians surrendered and thus North Africa was cleared of the enemy, which was wonderful news. However it riled us that we who had fought so hard and bitterly in 1941 and 1942 were denied this final accolade of triumph.

Morale was pretty low with this boredom, being out of action and these damned letters, etc. and we then really reached rock-bottom when we were told that we were not going to get the new Sherman tank after all. In fact we were not going to get any tanks. There was a chronic manpower shortage in the ME, particularly in infantry, and we - a regular Battalion of the Royal Tank Regiment, battle tested and experienced - were going to be turned into a BRIC. This was a Beach Reinforcement Invasion Company and the job of a BRIC was that after an invasion had taken place and the initial area cleared then the BRIC would go in to handle stores for the advancing troops. This was simply incredible!

'A' and 'C' Squadrons were turned into sort of Ordnance troops handling supplies and munitions - or as the men bitterly described it as 'bloody coolie labour work.' 'B' Squadron, however, had the best of a bad job as we were turned into and trained as an infantry company and this meant full training as infantry with rifle and bayonet, bren guns, mortars, etc.

*   *   *

There were occasional diversions. One day the CO called me in to his office and said that I was to go down to GHQ in Cairo to collect some Secret and Confidential documents, which I believe concerned the proposed attack on the island of Rhodes. This attack, however, was cancelled, most fortunately as is demonstrated later in this narrative.

I would be down there for about two or three days and as I was most utterly brassed off with what we were doing, or rather what we were not doing, I was happy to get away and took this as a splendid opportunity to let rip and enjoy myself to the full in the Cairo fleshpots as I was full of self-pity and feeling pretty miserable with life.

One morning, walking off a hangover, I found myself outside one of the big General Base Hospitals, the 64th I think, and on an impulse went in to find if there were any 8th RTR patients.

There were three, two of whom I cannot now remember who were well on their way to recovery and who would soon be rejoining us, but the third was Sgt. B— of one of the other squadrons. I will not name him just in case distant relatives who read this could be upset.

His tank had been knocked out at Alamein and he had suffered severe burns to most of his body. He was in another ward and I was warned that he was in a pretty bad way.

It was a huge ward and he was right down at the far end and I approached him rather apprehensively, and was appalled when I saw him.

His bed was in the corner and he was literally strung up, with his arms stretched out wide above his head, hanging from the ceiling, and his legs were similarly spread out and tied down to the bed corners. He had been burnt all over his body, though fortunately his face was OK, and his hands were bandaged to prevent him from tearing at his bandages owing to the pain and irritation he was experiencing.

I found it difficult to speak to him easily, and stupidly I offered him a cigarette which I put between his lips. When I bent forward and flicked my lighter he instinctively jerked his head back and dropped it, and I silently cursed myself for my crass stupidity and insensitivity as I remembered, too late, the fear and horror I myself experienced at the sight and feel of naked flame when I had been laid up from burns in a tank accident before the war and was in hospital for three months or so. Even today, after 56 years, I am still terrified by fire and its effects. I should, of course, have lit it and then given it to him.

I asked if there was anything I could get him or write any letters but he said that the nurses and other patients were wonderful and of great help in this respect. I stayed with him as long as decently possible and when I left I found the nearest toilet and retched my guts out.

Here I was, fit as a fiddle, bursting with good health, playing bags of sport, swimming etc. and enjoying life to the full, yet moaning at my 'misery' and misfortune - whereas the sights I had just seen in that hospital with all those wounded men, and in particular Sgt. B—, well, it just made me feel so thoroughly ashamed of myself. I was taught a salutary lesson that morning.

Incredibly and unbelievably he not only recovered but was passed as A1 by some damned medical board for further active service, and he came back to us but was tragically killed in the first week of the Gothic Line battle in Italy in 1944.

How he had the guts to come back and carry on as a Troop Sergeant once more after this horrific experience - well I just don't know. Another who did this was Captain Nick Moss of 'A' Squadron who had been badly burnt on his hands and face with the 5th RTR in the Desert, and others had been wounded more than once such as Hickey Sugden and Peter Kitto, who was tragically killed in a riding accident after being wounded three times. The medical boards must have been completely insensitive, heartless, and/or brutal to do this sort of thing and only God knows how they could possibly justify their actions.

Sergeant N—, of my Squadron and an old desert hand, was badly brewed-up in the last stages of the Gothic Line battle and when he eventually came back to report to me for duty (again, A1) I asked him if he would like to go back to his old Troop. He answered with scarcely any hesitation "Yes, of course Sir," however I told him that another sergeant had taken over and was doing a damn good job. I went on to say that I needed a good NCO in charge of the 'A' and 'B' Echelon transport and that I wanted him to do this if it was OK with him.

I am sure he was quite unaware of the wave of relief which went over his face as I said that, being quite ready to go back in at the sharp end once more, but fortunately I had enough common sense to realise that he had had quite enough by then and that he had more than earned a break.

This, however, was the calibre of men we were fortunate enough to have in the 8th RTR - men who were prepared cheerfully to do more than just their 'bit' and go on doing it time after time. Talk about guts and courage. I would dearly like to have been able to put some of those bastards on those boards who were responsible for those A1 gradings up the bloody sharp end themselves and to see just how much they liked it and how much they could take.

*   *   *

One amusing incident happened during this unhappy period and I chuckle even now when thinking about it. An Indian battalion - The Jaipurs - had recently arrived in the Middle East down in the Canal Zone and they were going to be put through their paces to carry out a night attack against enemy positions and the enemy in this case was to be 'B' Squadron. I was briefed as to what to expect from them and what I was expected to do and given maps of the area we were to defend, so I went out on a recce beforehand to get a good look at positions where the 'battle' was to take place.

I knew that I was meant to hold certain areas which were so marked on the map so that the Jaipurs could properly attack these particular positions, but I was damned if I was going to make it too easy for them, so, to make it more realistic, I recce'd one or two more which were not so marked on the map.

We moved up to our battle area about eight or nine pm that night, got properly dug in and waited for their attack. We had been issued with blank ammunition and thunder-flashes, Verey lights, etc. and I impressed on the Squadron to put up a determined resistance and to be as realistic as possible.

The Jaipurs came up and attacked somewhere round about 1am as far as I can remember, the night being clear but rather dark. Being inexperienced they rather gave themselves away with excited chattering and unnecessary noise and occasionally shouting out a battle cry, which might sound blood curdling, but gave away their positions and when they came to the top of the ridge and attacked the main force, after some spirited work, the Squadron surrendered itself whilst a few moved back to other positions which the Jaipurs hadn't expected.

I therefore made them push further forward than they had meant to and then, when they thought that they had finally mopped up 'the enemy,' they just sat around chattering and laughing and doing nothing else whilst their officers all got together in a group. I had expected this and I was in a sort of foxhole which was covered with a ground-sheet which had sand and stones etc. on top. I had with me a Bren-gunner, who of course had blank ammunition, but I had a couple of genuine '69' grenades. These were real grenades with plastic cases and generally used in close quarter fighting. I crept up closely to the group of officers, quite unseen, and threw both grenades which, unfortunately, were far too close and too accurate, at them, and they both exploded with a colossal bang! on either side of the group at the same time as my Bren-gunner raked them with a long burst. As one they all dived flat on their bloody faces!

When I went in the next day to hand in my report of their attack to the Infantry Training School CO I got the most phenomenal rocket from him and he told me emphatically that 'under no circumstances whatsoever would I ever use live ammunition - repeat never use live ammunition again in an exercise.'

He then chortled like hell and said that I had put the fear of God up the whole bloody lot of them, including himself (!), and that of course they should have started consolidating and preparing for the inevitable counter-attack. However all was forgiven and it had been most practical and useful and had really taught the Jaipurs something - "now come and have a drink!"

Our CO 'Bam' was rather unfairly blamed for this BRIC nonsense. It was not his fault - and unbeknown to us he stuck his neck out on a limb because he was a regular officer and he wrote to everybody he knew and pulled every string he could possibly think of - I believe he even wrote to the King who was Colonel Commandant of the Royal Tank Regiment - in an effort to get the 8th Tanks back with tanks and at long last the Powers-that-be agreed that we should be trained and equipped with the new Sherman tank.

*   *   *

The stupid things one does when young...

As I have said, this was an unhappy time for us and it didn't need much of an excuse to have some sort of a party. We had been training pretty hard down in the Kabrit area in the Canal Zone and were having a good lunch time session when Ian Gray suddenly challenged me to a swimming race across the canal, which was, I suppose a good half mile wide.

We changed into swimming trunks and were off. About half-way I realised that I was pretty 'blown' and turned round to suggest to Ian that we should swim back.

I couldn't see him anywhere and then his hands came up - or were going down - for about the second time and he was about ten yards or so behind me.

Somehow I managed to get him to the far bank, put him on his stomach with his face to one side and started to pump him like mad. Eventually he gurgled and spluttered and I lay down beside him utterly whacked.

Fortunately the others had seen what had happened and got hold of a small boat and picked us up. It could so easily have turned into a stupid tragedy.

On another occasion I had been swimming on my own and was sitting on a jetty consisting of wooden planking on scaffolding poles about 25-30 feet in length and had my feet dangling in the water at the end of it.

A chap was coming in at a pretty fast clip in a sailing dinghy - whether he was coming in to tie-up or just turn about I didn't know - but anyway, he suddenly realised that he was going too fast and did a smart tack-about.

He clouted the end of the jetty and knocked me into the water and I fell in amongst the scaffolding poles which were, of course, covered in rust and barnacles and had rough edges.

I was simply covered all over my arms, legs and chest with nasty scratches and looked as if I was suffering from 'the death of a 1,000 cuts!'

I had to go and have immediate attention and cursed like hell when I was covered in iodine, etc. I never did find out who was responsible and it was just as well that I didn't otherwise I would have murdered the bloody lunatic.

We then moved on, for some unknown reason, up into Syria, up near Baalback or Wadi Latrun up in the Bekka Valley and our CO and Second-in-Command, the Adjutant and all the Squadron Commanders were sent on an important conference to Cairo, I think about this new re-equipping, and so for one week as I was the Senior Captain I commanded the Regiment and my pride was very much dented when a most odd thing happened. It would.

The Sanitary Corporal, I think one called Corporal 'Dutchie' Holland, was an old regular and a very good type he was at his job. His truck caught fire and it destroyed the spare wheel and the camouflage netting, so he was up on a charge in front of me to explain how and why this had happened. Supplies of any description were exceptionally hard to get hold of and the destruction of the tyre was a most heinous crime with rubber being terribly short. He was allowed to use petrol to swab out the interior of the lorry to get rid of the filth accumulated and I asked him if any of the men had been smoking whilst they had been doing the job but he vehemently protested and said, "no." He said that the reason for the fire was that when two of the chaps jumped out to have a smoke and two more men jumped in to carry on cleaning it out the metal heel caps of their boots sparked on the metal floor of the truck and as it was still damp with petrol it just went up with a 'whoosh.' Before they had time to get the fire extinguisher out, the spare wheel and the camouflage net had been destroyed. On reflection this seemed like a perfectly natural explanation to me and so I dismissed the case as an accident.

About 16 months later when we were going through Italy and 'B' Squadron was right up the sharp end, enduring an extremely unpleasant shelling and mortaring, some mail came for me and in the mail was a buff envelope, I think marked OHMS, and I opened it wondering what the hell it was. It was a very severe rocket from some ruddy clerk in the War Office back in England who said that they had looked at the evidence and considered that my judgement was entirely wrong and as a result of it I would have to pay the cost of the tyre and the net, something like £5-17s-9d would be deducted from my pay and I was extremely lucky not to be on a charge myself for a gross dereliction of duty. You can rather imagine my language at the reception of the letter.

In another rugger game against a tough Australian XV I tackled hard one of their chaps, as did Charles 'Batty' Attwood (he would) at the same time. I knocked out two of Charles's teeth, hurting my hand, so that he got up clasping a hand to his mouth, which was bleeding, and I was hopping about with my hand in my armpit. The Aussie just got up and carried on with the game.

I went on leave that evening with John Herbertson to Tel Aviv and whilst in the bar noticed that my hand was all swollen and hurting like hell. Doc Leslie Milton was drinking with us and he said he would fix it for me. He asked for some hot water, very hot, and a compress and then got two of the chaps to hold my hand down on the bar-counter as he put on the compress which was boiling hot. I very nearly hit the roof! On return from leave five days later, as my hand was still painful and swollen I reported to Leslie. He looked at it and said, "You silly bugger! You should have gone to hospital as you have fractured your finger."

One day we had a lecture from a Captain Miller, an Australian, who had been captured and escaped. It was most interesting and he showed us some escape equipment which we could have and use if ever we were put in the bag: a) Silk maps which could be sown into our berets or shoulder tabs. b) Fly button compasses. c) Files to sew into shoulder tabs, etc.

A few days later I was in Tel Aviv and in the evening, in the Officers' Club, I met his younger brother who was a private and what he was doing in the Officers' Club I wouldn't know. He had escaped twice and he must have been an 'awkward type' of POW for the Gestapo bound his hands with barbed wire whilst he was in transit, in a train, being moved from an Italian POW Camp to a camp in Germany. (He showed me the awful scars on his wrists). He did the classic escape, asking his Italian Guard if he could go to the toilet and whilst in there he just heaved himself out through the window, whilst on the move, and rolled down a bank into some trees and bushes. He eventually got in with some Partizani group and then back to our lines and hence to the Middle East again.

One morning I was told that our CO 'Bam' wanted to see me and I thought, "Oh Lord! What 'black' had I put up this time," because, as I have already said, we were going through a very unhappy phase. Although I was playing a lot of sport: rugger, hockey, football and even some athletics I was drinking rather more than I should in the evenings.

'Bam' said to me, "Ham I have two things to discuss with you. I notice you are drinking rather a lot these days and it's damn silly of you, although I know the reason why, and I want you to stop it. The second thing is - Brigade have been requested to send a senior Captain with plenty of tank fighting experience to go as an Instructor to America to teach the Yanks about tank fighting." "Oh Boy!" I thought, "what a fantastic job and I will be able to get out of this miserable place we are in," and my morale shot up and I was in a state of euphoria. However I came back to earth with a jerk as I realised 'Bam' was still speaking and he said, "The Regiment is going through a very sticky patch and everyone is very unhappy - you know it and I know it. As you are one of the originals and as I know how you feel about the Regiment, and in particular, your own Squadron it is up to you and chaps like you to pull your weight and help it through this period. So I have told Brigade that I have already spoken to you about this posting and that you wish to decline it. So someone else from another Regiment is going in your place. This is all I have to say to you and remember what I said about your behaviour."

As I walked away my thoughts were very jumbled as, initially, the thought of going to America sounded absolutely marvellous, but 'Bam' was quite right as regards my feelings about the Regiment. He was being blamed, rather unfairly for our unhappiness as it was not his fault but just a question of circumstances and, as I have already mentioned, he did put his neck out in doing his best to get us taken off the blasted 'Brick' job and get us back to our proper role as a Tank Regiment.

Shortly after this I went down to Abbaysia Barracks to go on a 75mm gunnery course. I was so enthusiastic about this beautiful gun on the Sherman tank that I apparently got top marks and as a result of this I was made Gunnery Officer for the Regiment - very much to Charles 'Batty' Attwood's disgust as he wanted that job. I had on my desk in the Squadron office the nose cone of the 2-pounder shot and the nose cone of the 15-pound 75 millimetre shot and I think the difference in size astonished everybody. Particularly when I pointed out that this is what we had had slung at us in the desert and this was what we were now going to sling back, so that at least we would be on an equal footing with the damn Jerries.

I had an extraordinary lucky escape when we were practising a combined operation scheme down in the Canal Zone, somewhere near Kabrit, rehearsing disembarking from an assault ship at night. We were actually rehearsing for a combined op. to attack and land on the island of Rhodes but thank God! we never did it as the Jerries got wind of it and caused considerable casualties to a reconnaissance party which went over earlier so the operation was cancelled.

It was pitch dark and about 2am and we were told to embark on our landing craft which were swung out over the side of the main assault ship. I was fully kitted out with haversack, gas-mask, steel helmet, binoculars, revolver belt, compass and ammo, etc. and was standing at the edge of the deck looking down into the landing craft which was full of 'B' Squadron men.

It was all meant to be done with the minimum of noise and talking, and there were two or three sailors talking and larking about next to me. I angrily turned round and told them to shut up making so much noise and one of them spun round, lost his balance, flung out his arm and knocked me overboard. I hit the very edge of the landing craft, which was about ten-12 feet below the deck, landing half-on and half-off and fortunately someone grabbed my legs and prevented me from falling into the lake water which was about 30 feet below.

I was completely knocked-out and taken back to the sick-bay and had a couple of cracked ribs which were very sore and painful for some time afterwards. I very much doubt that if I had gone into the 'drink' laden as I was and unconscious at that, whether I would have survived.

One other rather amusing thing happened here, before we finally got equipped with the Shermans, when we held a gymkhana whilst we were somewhere up in the Raff-Gaza area. Ian Gray MC, one of the Squadron officers, was a bit of a dab hand on a horse and he entered the first race. I naturally put 50 piastres, which was about ten shillings, on him, and to my surprise and his surprise and everybody else's surprise he won. In the second race there was one of the gunnery instructors I had known at Abbaysia so I put the winnings on him and he won and in actual fact I won seven races out of seven and I was about £15 or £20 up, which was a hell of a lot of money in those days. The final race was a relay between the Palestine Mounted Police and the Tenth Hussars, so I naturally put the whole of my winnings on the Tenth Hussars and the bloody fools lost. That put me off betting for life.

One final memory of Palestine was a very pleasant one for me and is sheer boasting but I must include it. We had a very good rugger team and we played a Battalion of the Welsh Regiment, who I believe were undefeated at that time, and to our great delight we beat them six points to three. There were only three points, in those days, awarded for a try and guess who got the winning try, yes yours truly did! I certainly got plastered that night.

On the final run down from Palestine back into Egypt to pick up all our new Sherman tanks we stopped near the canal bank opposite

Ismailia and, knowing that there was a good Officers' Club there, I got hold of a jeep and piled three or four of 'B' Squadron officers into it to go and have a good night out. Petrol was in very short supply those days so that one had to have authority for any sort of journey so imagine my dismay when we came to a Bailey Bridge to cross the canal and found about a dozen or more vehicles stopped at the bridge entrance by a couple of MP's together with a red-capped Sergeant-Major.

I, of course, had no such authority and shouldn't be driving anyway so the officers said, "Ham! What the hell are we going to do now?" "Leave it to me," I said, and pulled out of the column and roared up to the Sergeant-Major. I told him that we were on the move down to the Canal Zone, moving off at dawn the next morning, and that I needed to go to the DPM (Deputy Provost Marshal) for movement orders so where was his office? I also explained that the other officers with me were to act as movement control for the Regimental convoy. He was a very tough looking character and he looked me up and down but gave me the necessary directions, stood back, saluted smartly and then said, "The Officers' Club is in the same street and only about 200 yards away from his office - have a good evening Sir." He was obviously an old desert veteran and I think that he realised I was one also and I am sure that is why he let us through.

It was absolutely wonderful to be re-equipped once again as a complete Tank Regiment with the super new Sherman tank and our morale was simply sky high.

The 8th Army had by now successfully taken Sicily and had moved on into Italy itself and we guessed that this was to be our objective at last.

3
Italy 1944-1945

The year started well because on 4th January we moved down to Fayid in the Canal Area in Egypt and joined the 7th Armoured Brigade.

This Brigade then consisted of the 2nd, the 6th and the 8th RTR - three regular RTR regiments in one armoured brigade - this was quite unique and I think it was the only time it happened during the war. We were very proud to wear the famous Desert Rat insignia of the 7th Armoured Brigade, showing a Jerboa on our sleeves and on our vehicles.

The reason for creating this elite armoured brigade will be mentioned later on in this narrative. For the next three months we trained really hard: firing on the range, manoeuvres, practising close co-operation with infantry and guns etc. We were all 100% fit and trained and, as I have already indicated, morale was absolutely sky high.

On 23rd March I left the Regiment to go to Italy in advance of them to go on a special course. I arrived at Naples I think about five days later, and here two rather rotten things happened to me.

First of all my black tin trunk, which had all my worldly possessions including precious bottles of whisky, brandy, cigarettes, silver hip flask, photographs of my wife etc. went missing and exhaustive searches failed to find it. I found out approximately two years later what happened. It had somehow got mixed up with equipment for the Polish Corps and had travelled with them all over Italy and was eventually sent back to base in Cairo who then forwarded it to Bovington Camp, the RTR Depot in Dorset, and eventually it reached me at my in-laws' house in April 1946 when I was on my demobilisation leave.

One morning a British Railways lorry drew up outside their house and a very battered tin trunk was delivered, secured with masses of rope, and when I opened it I found that not a single item was missing!

This speaks volumes for the honesty of the Poles and the various people who handled it in transit and I think that the whisky, brandy, cigarettes, razor blades and so on were every bit as valuable then, if not more so, as rationing was extremely strict in England immediately after the war. Prudently I had insured its contents with an insurance company in Egypt for about £47 or so but I very much regret to say that I did not refund the claim cheque which they had issued to me in 1944 - so my own standards were sadly lacking.

I went to a Transit Camp before going on my course and here an extremely distasteful incident occurred.

The Adjutant of the camp came in one evening and said that all captains with moustaches were to report to the ante-room and about five or six of us trooped in. I asked him what the hell it was in aid of and he replied that there was to be an identity parade because a young Italian boy had been indecently assaulted some weeks ago. I most indignantly protested saying that I had only just arrived and he replied, with a smile, that he knew that but it was purely an identity parade so I had nothing to worry about.

We lined up and a few minutes later a sweating captain of, I think, Ordnance was marched in and unfortunately he was placed next to me. He looked very pale and was perspiring profusely and then a young Italian boy, of about ten or 12 years old, came in with an Italian interpreter and a Military Police Officer. The boy was then asked to walk up and down the line of officers and to pick out and identify the man who had assaulted him. The young boy looked extremely nervous and apprehensive and he then said something to the interpreter who gabbled back at him so he walked up and down again and turned once more to the interpreter and, to my horror, he hesitantly lifted his hand and pointed at me, shrugging his shoulders as he did so. This of course was the end of the parade and the boy left the room and the chap next to me damn nearly passed out as he was led away. I felt physically unclean and went back into the mess and had several stiff drinks.

This time I found out where my brother was stationed and it was just outside Naples. I managed to contact him by telephone and he came over and picked me up as I was allowed two or three days leave before my course started. I told him how much I would like to have a look at the famous Monte Cassino so he got out his truck and the two of us went to have a look at it.

When it came into sight I was awed by its sheer magnificence and impressiveness and realised what a hell of a place it would be to attack and capture. We carried on motoring and I mentioned to him that things seemed to be very quiet, which was an unfortunate remark to make at that particular moment.

The road was on quite an embankment and the precise moment I spoke two American 155mm guns let fly a salvo when we were right alongside them and I nearly went through the roof of the truck as this was so unexpected and the first time that I had heard anything fired in anger for just over a year.

We then became aware of several soldiers frantically waving at us from trenches at the side of the road and my dear elder brother suddenly realised that he had come simply miles too far up near the sharp end and he very hastily did a smart turnabout and shot out of the area like a bat out of hell. However, he still argues today that he was not then lost but merely trying to give me a grandstand view of Cassino and protests at my 'brotherly ingratitude'! I still say "rubbish!"

Whilst staying with my brother a friend of his, Captain Tim Gobey, suggested that we should try our hands at a spot of bird shooting as he had a couple of shotguns, so we went out to some nearby woods.

There seemed to be very few birds around and we were not very successful, but eventually I managed to wing a pigeon and it fell near to us.

When we picked it up I felt pretty rotten to see its blood spattered little body and even more apprehensive when I noticed a metal tag around one of its legs, marked clearly US Air Corps, though most fortunately it was not carrying a message.

I have never ever shot a bird or animal since that day as it seemed to me such a cruel and heartless 'sport' with all the stupid slaughter going on all around us.

*   *   *

On April 8th I moved up to Benevento to start my three week course on Close Support of All Arms, eventually rejoining the Regiment in early May. I found out that whilst I had been in Italy the 8th RTR had had to surround a Greek brigade in the desert as they had rebelled, or something like that, having a strong Communist element in it, and order had to be restored. Whilst travelling fast in a Dingo Scout Car, Leo Stock from 'B' Squadron had slid off the road and was killed when the Dingo overturned. This was a tragic and stupid loss of a good bloke.

The Regiment had left Egypt on April 29th and landed at Taranto on May 4th. When I rejoined the Squadron it more or less coincided with Robbie's 26th birthday and this naturally had to be celebrated in some style, so we went into the Officers' Club in, I think, Lanciano.

Robbie then ordered 26 bottles of wine (!) between about seven of us, which we then had to demolish, at least we tried to do so. Quite naturally he got completely sloshed, as did most of us.

When we got back to camp he had passed out in the back of the truck so Ian Gray and I got his six-foot three-inch frame out, draped his arms round our shoulders and tried to get him into his tent. He kept coming to and trying to stand up which made it very difficult for Ian and I, as we were pretty far gone ourselves, so that we all kept falling down.

I think that we crashed into every single tent in the Squadron area - and some of them more than once - before we finally found his own and judging from the startled oaths and various obscenities from their occupants we were not very popular that night. I don't think that Robbie was seen again for at least 36 hours...

When Robbie got plastered his eye-balls used to protrude so that he looked like that old comic actor Mischa Auer, whereas Ian Gray, who was small and dark - well his eyes used to go back into his head so that he looked like a slit-eyed Chinaman.

When Johnnie Herbertson joined us later as my second in command in the Squadron, on getting into the same state I swear that his forehead used to beam just like a lighthouse.

If, therefore, the three of them were together like this then it had the most bizarre effect so that one would have to reach for the bottle oneself, with a shaking hand, muttering, "My God! I need a drink..."

Before rejoining the 8th RTR I managed to get attached for a few days to the 40th RTR, who had been in Italy for some time then, and was able to learn quite a lot from them of their fighting experiences which would be of use to us in the future. I also managed to track down and spend a day with our old Brigadier 'Boomer' Watkins DSO who was then in charge of Tank Delivery and Tank Reinforcements.

He had quite a small office and staff and in his deep and rather sepulchral voice he explained that he felt somewhat out of things being "one of the back room boys as it were." I told him how much I was in awe of him when I joined his Brigade HQ back in the UK in 1940, when I was a brand new second lieutenant. He laughed delightedly when I reminded him of the story when we crossed The Wire in November 1941 at night and he suddenly appeared like magic out of the darkness and saved my bacon as he was able to direct me to the 8th RTR HQ as he had just left them - as I was hopelessly lost. He had quite forgotten this incident and it amused him greatly. The Western Desert campaign must have been pretty rough for him because it was a war of movement - very rapid movement at times - and living conditions were pretty stark and, after all, he was a World War One veteran. He was a nice old boy and I am glad that I called in to see him.

*   *   *

There could hardly have been a greater contrast between war in the Desert and the war in Italy - totally different terrain, tanks and tactics.

In the Desert we had the Valentine tank which was small, slow, had only a three-man crew and was armed with a piddling little 2-pdr popgun: in Italy however we had the Sherman which was fast as it could crack along at 25-30 mph, it had a five-man crew which meant that the tank commander could at long last do his job properly, and, above all, it had a superb 75mm gun which was very accurate and could fire a 15lb shell some six-and-a-half miles and its 15lb solid armour-piercing shot could do real damage to the German tanks at last. In addition it had two .30 Browning machine-guns, another .50 Browning machine-gun on the tank commander's cupola ring and a 2" mortar on the side of the turret.

In a Squadron of 16 tanks one had therefore 16 x 75mms; 32 x .30 machine-guns; 16 x .50 machine-guns and 16 x 2" mortars which was really quite some fire power in those days.

It did, however, have two drawbacks, the first of which was its height as the top of the turret was some 11 feet off the ground. It was not easy therefore to conceal oneself behind hedges or underneath trees, in fact we were rather apt to stick out like a sore thumb.

The other disadvantage was that the armour was pretty thin as it was only about two-and-a-half inches thick and as we were sitting on about 100 rounds of 75mm - mostly high explosive - and 90 gallons of petrol - and up to 5,000 rounds of .30 Browning machine-gun ammo - well, we were like a travelling incinerator. The German anti-tank guns could easily penetrate it at long range but it was extremely reliable and we loved it after the Valentine.

We were then in the region somewhat to the west of Ortona and after 15 or 16 months of being out of action it was a bit strange when in leaguer at night, lying in one's small tent, hearing the whistle and

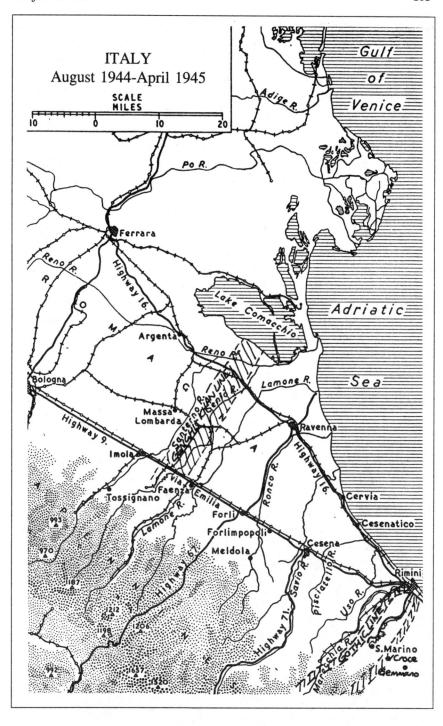

ITALY
August 1944-April 1945

SCALE
MILES

crump of shells as they landed in the leaguer area and it was extraordinary the number of duds which seemed to come over, thank God, which gave rise to the rumour that this was sabotage on the part of the slave labour in the Third Reich who were responsible for these munitions. We went out on various shoots to help out the infantry and one particular one I remember very clearly indeed.

The whole area had been subjected to quite heavy enemy shell fire and the higher command was getting a bit fed up about this so it was decided to have a retaliation shoot. I think something like a battery of 155 millimetre 'Long Toms' plus two batteries of 25-pounders and two Squadrons of ourselves were laid on to do a shoot on a certain German position right on the coast.

We had all ranged on to the area at different times and Intelligence had reported back that the Germans, being very methodical, used to have a bathing parade followed by a pay parade on a Wednesday about midday and it was decided that this 'stonk' should coincide with their pay day, so at 12.00 hours on this particular Wednesday the whole damned lot of us opened up with about ten minutes gun fire. Goodness knows what the result was but an enormous cloud of dust was seen to rise in the air and it was noticeable that the shelling of our positions died down very considerably after that.

When we came back in the evening to refuel and re-ammo one of the tanks somehow caught fire and Captain Robinson MC (Robbie) showed considerable initiative and coolness when he jumped into the driver's seat and drove it out of the leaguer area. He said afterwards that he thought this was the right thing to do to get it away in case the damn thing blew up and set fire to other tanks in the leaguer. The fire was eventually put out and the tank was not seriously damaged and it was a good effort on his part.

Shortly after this we started to move up towards the battle area, the Regiment being moved on train-flats, and I was in charge of the party. We stopped en route at some small village the name of which I can't remember and as we had to wait for about half-an-hour I decided to walk in and see what it looked like. I came across a disabled Sherman tank in the little piazza, the crew of which were working on the engine and tracks. The sergeant tank commander came up to me, looking rather worried, and said that he and the crew were being harried by a group of drunken Partizani who kept coming up and interfering with the crew whilst they were working at repairing the tank.

Just before I had arrived one of the Partizani came over and his driver, who was a small but very muscular Scotsman, irritatedly pushed him out of the way. The Italian then suddenly turned on him and bit him quite badly on the shoulder and his ear, whereupon the Jock gave him a beautiful right upper-cut and knocked him out cold. This seemed to enrage the other Partizanis and, as they were drinking heavily and noisily at the Taverna across the other side of the piazza, the Sergeant was getting rather uptight about the situation.

I told him to get hold of his tommy-gun and ordered the crew to train the 75mm gun on the Taverna and then the Sergeant and I walked over to it. The inn-keeper could speak a bit of English and I could, by then, speak a little bit of Italian and I told him, very angrily, that he was to close the Taverna immediately and that no more drinks were to be served until the British troops arrived in the area and that they would be up shortly that evening. He protested vigorously, as did one of the Partizani whom I presumed to be their leader, so, in a rather theatrical gesture I swept all the bottles and glasses off the tables and they crashed onto the pavement. I then turned and raised my arm to the gunner in the Sherman at the back of the piazza. Prior to that I had told him that if I did that then he was to open fire with the turret Browning machine-gun, firing in the air over the top of the Taverna. This he did to the consternation of everyone who went down flat on their bloody faces. When the inn-keeper got up I angrily told him that he had exactly five minutes - "cinque minute" - to close the damn place down and, if he didn't, the 75mm "grande cannone" would open fire and blow the Taverna to pieces.

The Sergeant and I then turned round and marched back to his tank. This was the only thing that I could do for this unfortunate crew because we, the 8th RTR, were moving off almost immediately afterwards and I can only hope that it had the desired effect. The Sergeant seemed pretty pleased and impressed by the demonstration, as were, I hope, the inhabitants of this little village.

Shortly after this incident a very unfortunate accident occurred when we were moving up further towards the line, on our tracks this time. We were approaching a small town or village and the local Partizani, who had been drinking and were waving bottles as well as flags, stopped us to lead us in. I lent forward and ordered my driver to advance and, tragically, one of the Partizani whom I couldn't see as he was behind me, tried to jump up onto the tank at the same time. His leg got caught in the track and was badly mangled before we could stop.

It was a nasty wound, his thigh being very badly and deeply cut almost to the bone so we gave him what medical aid we could, ie some morphia and field dressings and then lifted him up onto the back to take him into the town. Another Partizani jumped up screaming dementedly, "Mia fratello! Mia fratello!" (my brother! my brother!) so we took him along as well. When we got into the town there were hundreds of excited Italians, shouting, waving flags, etc. and I had to bellow out at the top of my voice, "Dove dottore? Dove dottore? subito! subito!" (Where is a doctor? quickly!). He was tenderly lifted down and I gave his brother some more morphine, bandages, etc. as they took him away. This was all that I could do for him and I hope he survived OK but it was a very nasty wound. Once again a most extraordinary incident occurred to me about a week or two later and I think that it was the most moving experience that I have ever had.

We were moving up forward and found that the road had been blown and the area mined so Peter Butt, my Squadron Commander, told me to try and find a suitable detour through some fields so I went off in my tank on my own. It was a very hot day and as we were going across a dry and dusty field I could see, at the far side of it, a few small farm outbuildings and group of about 30-odd people by the buildings. As we got nearer I saw that most of them were elderly, with a few excited children, and they were waving flags and shouting, "Viva Ingelaise! Viva Ingelaise! Viva!" I ordered my driver to halt and jumped down to speak to them and they all crowded around me then they suddenly went quiet and pulled back as, round the corner, came an old priest wearing incredibly ancient clothes. In fact his habit was so old that it was almost rusty green in colour as opposed to being black.

He was unshaven, his face the colour and texture of a wrinkled old walnut, his breath stank of garlic and I could see through his old cracked shoes that he was not wearing any socks. He came up to me and gave me a lovely smile and then, turning to the little group of people, he told them to come closer and then go down on their knees. He closed his eyes and intoned a prayer, making the sign of the cross with his hand above their heads and with my limited Italian I could understand that he was obviously thanking God for their deliverance. When he finished he then turned round and walked past me to my tank and sprinkled it with Holy Water, making the sign of the cross on its front, and then he came back to me and gestured that I should kneel. I did this, quickly removing my dusty beret, and he liberally sprinkled me with Holy Water so that it ran down my face and stained my dusty overalls. He made the sign of the cross on my forehead, murmuring a prayer as well, which I understood to be for my safety.

I felt incredibly moved by this and as I stood up I tried to say something appropriate in my halting Italian. He smiled once more and spoke rapidly to a small boy who grinned and disappeared round the side of one of the buildings. He reappeared with a battered tin tray on which were some glasses and about half-a-dozen cups - they were that poor. He then turned to me once more, grinning, and I could see his blackened teeth and a strong whiff of garlic came up and I thought, "Oh my God! He's going to kiss me!" But, Thank Heavens! he didn't and instead he put his hand inside his habit, explaining in broken English, "Capitano! Theese I save. Journo grande! Journo magnifico!" and produced a beautiful bottle of Napoleon brandy! Bottles of vino then appeared as if by magic amongst the small crowd and the crew and I had quite a good celebratory little session.

We continued to move up slowly with very slight opposition, chiefly blown roads, bridges, etc. with the odd spot of mortar and shell fire and one of the small places we 'liberated' was a lovely little hill-top town called Citta St. Angelo. Once again a rather moving little ceremony occurred, this would be around May/June 1944. A few days earlier the inhabitants realised that at last they were about to be liberated as the Germans were pulling out, so two of the town ladies had, very courageously, secretly made two flags - one being the Union Jack and the other the Stars and Stripes - out of whatever material they could find. Goodness knows what would have happened to them and others in this town if the Germans had ever found out about this. The local Partizani had also been distributing leaflets urging the townspeople to help the Allies as much as they could - showing where the roads, fields, bridges, etc. were mined and waiting for the great day of liberation.

On this particular morning, Peter Butt, my Squadron Commander and close friend, went up to the Town Square with Robbie and some half-a-dozen tank crew and there the Town Mayor and his wife, the two ladies and a few of the townsfolk attended a small ceremony in which the Mayor handed over the flags to Peter. It was a simple but rather moving ceremony and afterwards drinks in celebration were passed round. Today, those flags and a copy of the Partizani leaflet are with the 8th RTR memorabilia in the Tank Museum at Bovington Camp, Dorset.

We continued moving up closer to the sharp end and on one occasion when we were fairly close we were asked to help some infantry who were being harassed by very accurate shooting from German guns and mortars. They said that the German OP (Observation Post) together with some 81mm mortars were right up forward but that the 25-pdrs of ours had not been able to knock them out. They understood that the Sherman 75mm's were meant to be very accurate (which they were) and hoped that we might be able to do something about this.

I was told to see what I could do to help them so I went up to their front line positions, carefully marked out where the mortar positions were on my map, and in particular the enemy OP. He was called 'the man in the cage' because it was a hole on a forward slope of ground, surrounded with rocks and well camouflaged with nets, lattice work, etc. and very difficult to hit with artillery. I reported back to our RHQ and it was arranged that I should take a half-Squadron, i.e. two Troops of tanks, my own and a support tank, making a total force of eight, and move up forward and to go and deal with this. We moved up to about 800-1,000 yards behind the infantry positions and I moved further forward still and got Lance-Corporal Shapcott, my gunner, to range on the target. He was a damn good gunner and, after having bracketed it, his fourth or fifth shot appeared to be a direct hit and when he repeated his aim I said, "that's it." (The Sherman 75mm was extraordinarily accurate and one could put a round through the window or down through the door of a 'casa' at a good range - something the 25-pdrs couldn't do).

I had been carefully calibrating and calculating each shot and passing on the range and degrees, etc. to the other tanks, who had previously calibrated onto my 'master' gun, and, having said "that's it" I then gave the order for five rounds gun fire. As one we all let rip and some 40 shells plastered the position and we completely obliterated it. After that I gave the order for independent fire and the eight of us ranged all over the area shooting up the marked mortar positions, hedges, ditches, buildings, etc. giving the Jerries a really good pasting before moving back.

The infantry CO 'phoned up later to congratulate us saying that they were highly delighted with the result of the shoot as we had certainly knocked out 'the man in the cage' because some time later a German half-track flying a Red Cross symbol had gone to 'the cage' obviously to pick up casualties. We appeared to have demolished the mortar positions as well and we seemed to have shaken the Jerries alright as things were very much quieter all round and he couldn't have been more pleased with us. We were now very much nearer the sharp end of things and the situation of the two Armies requires elaborating.

The Gothic Line Battle, which was shortly to commence, was considered to be the bloodiest and the most bitter of the whole of the Italian Campaign and certainly both sides suffered heavy casualties. The line stretched from Pesaro on the Adriatic coast - our sector - westward to the mountains and then climbed north to Florence and continued north and west to reach the west coast somewhere around about Carrara. It was generally well prepared and strongly held and in depth anything from ten to 20 miles right across from east to west. Not only houses but complete small villages had been turned into strong points with wire, mines, dug-in infantry, guns, concreted machine-gun posts, and of course every single bridge and every crossing, road and mountain pass had been blown and mined. All these areas were under complete observation by the Germans holding the high ground so they could watch our slow tortuous advance from the south and literally plaster us with heavy concentrations of artillery fire.

The 8th Army was attacking on the right flank, which was the Adriatic coast, our sector, and to the mountains going west and further west the American 5th Army was attacking on the left flank. The 8th Army consisted then of some five corps, as follows: 5,10, New Zealand Corps, Polish and Canadian Corps, which meant that we had something like 12-14 Infantry Divisions and three Armoured Divisions on call. Opposite us was the German 10th Army, consisting of three Army Corps, together with three Italian Army Corps and this meant that they had also something like 10-12 Divisions in the field.

The battle was expected to follow roughly the pattern of the El Alamein battle, i.e. there would be very heavy and intensive fighting for about 10-12 days then the enemy would probably break and once that breakthrough had been achieved then there would be a strong armoured thrust right through, which would be spearheaded by the 7th Armoured Brigade (ourselves) which is why we had been formed - to do this particular job. Our orders would be to go smack through and across the south-east corner of the Romagna, from Rimini, up the Lombardi Plain to Bologna, some 70 miles away and then swing right up to Ferarra to cut their lines of communication and to create havoc and mayhem in their rear areas. A real Blitzkrieg effort. Unfortunately Higher Command's ambitions in this respect did not come off for two reasons. (A third reason will be revealed later in this text.)

The first was the determined and almost fanatical resistance the Germans put up in this battle. They resisted most tenaciously almost every single yard of ground so that our advance was very slow and very, very costly as this was virtually their last main line of defence south of the Alps. The 8th Army did not have the numerical superiority in infantry, which was essential and desperately needed, because General Alexander had, of course, had to send back many first class divisions of infantry and armour to England for the D-Day landings while the terrain here was absolutely soaking up infantry and armour like a sponge soaking up water. The second factor, which was cruelly unfortunate, was that by the time we had almost reached a break-through, which was towards the end of September - not 10-12 days but more like three to four weeks - the autumn rains started unnaturally early and the ground was turned into an absolute quagmire so any fast pursuit was absolutely out of the question.

On August 26th our Brigadier gave us a pep talk outlining the information given above and between the 27th and 29th we moved right up to the battle area and the battle for the Gothic Line started on August 31st. We were not in the forefront of the battle as naturally we, 7th Armoured Brigade, were being held back for the hoped-for breakthrough, but my diary does show that on September 1st we were in action and 'B' Squadron lost two tanks when Captain Dickinson and Sergeant Gordon were knocked out - fortunately both came back OK to our lines, but on September 6th we really came up against a very tough spot indeed. This was at Croce, and the name of this place and its memories probably sends a shiver down the backs of many infantry chaps who were there. It was one of the very strongly held and prepared villages with mines, wire, dug-in guns of every description all over the place and it was decided that as the infantry were having such a rough time the 2nd RTR would attack on the east, or right flank and pretty well right on down the main road and we, the 8th RTR, would attack on the left flank going up a narrow valley.

The valley was so narrow that it was almost impossible to deploy a two-Squadron front. On our right flank the ground was not good with ditches, hedgerows, buildings etc. and on our left the ground rapidly rose up into the mountains and the position was very strongly held indeed with mines, wire, dug-in guns and infantry. Of course with the Jerries on the mountain tops observing exactly where we were going and what we were doing the whole time, we came under extremely heavy concentrations of artillery and mortar fire and were just 'stonked' to blazes. It was absolutely chronic. I ordered my lap-gunner, Eric Mace, to fire his machine-gun at every damn hedge, ditch, thicket etc. and L/Cpl. Shapcott was similarly blasting away with the 75mm at any likely enemy positions and on more than one occasion we were rewarded with a sudden flare-up as we obviously hit ammunition, or a vehicle or something. However we were being plastered left, right and centre the whole time. It really was very rough indeed.

Shapcott fired with the 75mm at something but nothing happened so he yelled out "misfire." Carter, the gun loader, immediately whipped open the breech of the gun to eject the shell, as he thought, and quickly handed it up to me and as it was bloody hot I threw it out of the turret. Unfortunately it was not the complete shell but only the shell-case because it was not a misfire but a damned 'separated case,' which left 15lbs of high explosive jammed up the gun barrel. So what the hell was one to do under these difficult circumstances?

There was only one thing to do so poor old Joe Soap, myself, had to hop outside with all this carnage and corruption flying about, undo three six-foot lengths of cleaning-rod strapped to the side of the tank, go round to the gun, getting the gunner to depress it fully so that I could insert the cleaning-rod into the barrel and gently - oh! so very gently! - tap the offending 15lbs of high explosive back into the turret so that it could then be chucked out.

All the while I was petrified that if I hit it too hard I would set off the nose detonator which would be curtains for myself - to say nothing of the crew inside - let alone all the incredible amount of stuff which was flying all around outside. I got my leg pulled unmercifully by the Squadron afterwards when they asked what the hell was I doing cleaning my gun in the midst of a battle? I can assure you I was very pleased indeed to hop back inside the safety of the turret.

We hung around until it was dark, unable to proceed forward because we didn't have any infantry or artillery with us as it was all on the right flank supporting the 2nd RTR's attack into the village itself.

By the time it was dark we had to pull back to leaguer as we very urgently needed petrol and ammunition. The Regiment lost 19 tanks that day.

Whilst we were in the leaguer area Peter Butt and I walked around and on the road we came across an abandoned Sherman tank; it was not one of ours, presumably it was one of the 2nd RTR and Peter said he would hop up and have a look to see if anyone was inside the turret. So he grabbed hold of the barrel of the Browning machine-gun on the front of the tank to haul himself up and gave a yell as he did so because the damn thing fired one round and the shot went right across the palm of the glove he was wearing and through the sleeve of my jacket but didn't hurt either of us except to give us one hell of a fright.

Sergeant Condon, MM and Bar, did a very fine thing here. It was completely dark and we were just about settling down for the night when apparently he heard the sobbing and crying and moaning of a demented Italian woman who was wandering around in the dark in the battlefield and all sorts of things were going on, mortar shells, machine-gun fire and more. There were mines out there as well and so he quietly went out and got hold of her, and brought her back to safety. Quite what happened to her after that I don't know but knowing Condon I reckoned that he fixed up something that was satisfactory. Anyway, it was a very fine effort on his part. On September 8th we were then just about into the heart of the defensive area in our sector and the resistance was getting stronger all the time when we then came up against one hell of a position at Monte Gemmano. This was one of the key positions up here and it was a race against time as to who was to get up there first in any considerable strength.

At first light we were crawling up a mountain track with the mountain gradually petering away to our immediate right but an almost precipitous drop of some 1500-2000 feet to our left and the track was only wide enough to take one tank at a time. Sgt. Huxtable was in the lead and I was immediately behind him as we came round the top of the track and onto a small, flat, rocky plateau with Gemmano village about 600-800 yards away and looking very battered.

We moved forward slowly and warily and after about 300 yards I ordered him to halt as I didn't like the look of the place at all. I looked at it hard with my binoculars and there was no movement of any kind, it was unnaturally quiet and I felt we were walking into an absolute trap.

Suddenly, out of the corner of my eye, I saw a chap on my right who was waving as he came stumbling towards me - he was too tired to run - and a very exhausted officer of the 2/6 or 2/7 Queens came up to the side of my tank.

"For God's sake - Look Out! Jerry is holding out in there in some considerable strength and..." that was all he had time to say because from the ruins of the village there suddenly jumped up what seemed to be an enormously tall German soldier as he lifted a *Faust-petronnen* (anti-tank rocket launcher) to his shoulder and fired point blank at Sgt. Huxtable's tank which went up with a whoosh as it exploded into a ball of fire and oily, black smoke. I had halted immediately behind him and was only about 15 yards away and to his right and all the flames and smoke were blowing right across my line of vision.

I immediately ordered my driver to go into reverse and swing left to get to the left side of the burning tank and he knew, as the whole crew knew, and they hoped to God that I had remembered, that there was this precipitous drop to our immediate left. As soon as we were clear we opened up with everything we had for about a couple of minutes until I gave the order to cease fire.

Suddenly I noticed, to my horror, a pair of hands fluttering away in the top of the burning tank in front of me. "Christ!" I exclaimed, "that's Huxtable! Give me covering fire" and I immediately jumped out whilst Cpl. Shapcott tried to grab me by my legs as he shouted "You're not going out there Sir!" but I was away and breaking the 100 yards sprint record.

Huxtable was half out of the tank by the time I got to him and I managed to drag him out and get him onto the ground behind his tank. Somehow or other I got him back to my tank and the crew threw out the first aid kit and I dressed his burns as best I could and gave him a shot of morphia. I then told him to report back to Major Butt as fast as he could and to tell him what the situation was. He was a good man and although badly shocked he was compos mentis and off he went behind the edge of the plateau. I then realised that I had the very tricky job of getting back into my own tank and I knew that this was not going to be at all easy as a certain amount of stuff had been fired at me on the run and, as I have previously mentioned, the top of the blasted Sherman was about 11 feet off the ground. Moreover, I was in full view of the enemy and pretty well at point blank range.

I crawled up onto the back of the engine covers and crouched down behind the turret, which was itself about two-and-a-half feet high, and shouted out that I was going to count up to three and then say "coming in now" and as soon as I said that Mace, my front machine-gunner, was to open up for all he was worth and spray the general area immediately in front to keep the Jerries' heads down. Cpl. Shapcott would have to elevate the 75mm because there was no way that I could hop quickly into the turret through the very small Tank Commander's cupola with the 75mm level because the chute to catch the empty shell cases would be in the way of my legs and Boy! was I going to come in with one hell of a rush. I took a deep breath, counted up to three, and yelled out "Now" and jumped onto the top of the turret as Mace opened up - firing about three bloody rounds and then stopping. I found out afterwards that the idiot had forgotten to check his ammo-belt and he had run out of ammo. So, probably for about four or five seconds, I was on top struggling to get in, with no covering fire at all, at point blank range in full view of the enemy and naturally they opened up on me with a couple of Spandaus. I heard the "trrrrrr ttt" and felt a burning sensation right in my crutch as I fell into the turret, nearly breaking my left knee-cap as Shapcott was rapidly levelling the 75mm and clutching my matrimonials for all I was worth thinking "Christ! The bastards have got me - what a place to be hit!" Shapcott was blasting away now like mad and I was gingerly looking out over the top of the turret, still clutching myself, until there was so much smoke, dust and debris flying about from his firing that I had to order him to stop.

He did so and when it slowly cleared I suddenly saw a hand, then an arm and then a shoulder coming through the rubble and thought, "My God! That blasted Jerry's going to have a crack at us!" and sure enough, this very brave German soldier - we found out later that they were the 1st Paratroops up there, chaps who had been at Monte Cassino and very tough cookies indeed - jumped up once more and I could see him clearly as he was lifting his *Faust-Petronnen* to blast at us, but we fired first, and blew him to pieces with a direct hit from the 75mm. Things quietened down a bit after that and I was feeling a bit sick and it was hurting like hell down below so my gun loader, Curly Carter (bald as a coot!) impatiently said, "Come on Sir, drop 'em and let's have a shufti." I gingerly removed my hand from my crutch and looked down and saw, right at the top of my inner thighs, two jagged tears in my overall trousers but no blood, so I undid my revolver belt and dropped my trousers and there were corresponding tears in my khaki shorts but again, no blood, which I thought was a bit odd. I hesitated for a moment but Carter impatiently said, "Come on Sir, drop 'em" which I did and, quite frankly, I was afraid to look.

He bent down and looked at me fairly closely and then, with a look of bewilderment on his face, he looked up and said, "Sir, there's fuck all there." "My God!" I said in horror, "Have they shot 'em off?" Obviously they hadn't otherwise I wouldn't be here or at least I would be speaking in a high falsetto voice for the rest of my life and would have the full qualifications to join the Luton Girls Choir as a male soprano.

However, when I did look down I did find that right at the top of my thighs, on the inside, there were two angry, red burn marks where the machine-gun bursts had gone through my clothing and legs, grazing and burning the skin but not, thank God! penetrating. Talk about luck.

What had actually saved me was a modification I had got the fitters to carry out - to the tank and not to me - only a few days earlier. The Sherman had a 2" mortar mounted on the right hand side of the turret but of course this would only fire in the direction the turret was pointing. I got them to take it off and fit it to my turret cupola-ring so that I could fire it in any direction I required. It nearly broke my wrist each time I fired it but it was very useful to lob an HE or smoke shell at, or behind, a building when the turret was pointing in a different direction. The mounting was only about one-and-a-half or two inches wide and the bursts of Spandau machine-gun fire had hit it and splattered left and right through my legs.

There were no infantry at all in sight up there and we had no artillery support so I radioed back to Peter explaining this and to see if something could be done about it (there wasn't really enough room for another tank or two to come up in support as there was no cover whatsoever and they would be just like sitting ducks). He came back on the air to say that this was being arranged and hopefully soon, but damn all happened and I just had to stay up there for the rest of the day, firing, moving about, being fired at - just like an Aunt Sally sideshow, until it was almost dark. Eventually I was able to pull back once more behind the spur of the mountain and was I pleased to do this. 'B' Echelon came up that night to replenish us but of course they couldn't get their vehicles right up to us owing to the narrowness of the track, so everything had to be passed up by hand and it took hours to do this.

I suppose it must have been somewhere about 1am and a really beautiful night it was, warm and masses of stars in a cloudless sky. I was leaning against the front of my tank talking to Robbie and my driver, L/Cpl. Clayton, when suddenly without any warning whatsoever there was a brilliant flash right between my feet and the blast of the explosion blew us all over. It could only have been a mortar bomb as we never heard the Whoosh! from a shell. I got to my feet, holding my arm, as I had hit it very hard against something, or something had hit it, and I thought that I had broken my elbow as it was hurting like hell. Robbie, all 6'2" of him, was covered in dust and dusting himself down and swearing like mad. I was rubbing my arm whilst Corporal Clayton was standing with his hands covering his face and I noticed blood was trickling down them and when he took them away I found that his face was pitted with cuts from stones and gravel from the track, also that his eye was beginning to close, so I ordered him to go back down and have it seen to. He was a very good bloke and didn't want to go but I thought it was essential in case something had damaged his eye - in any case he was a bit shocked. Robbie and I were completely OK. We had a fairly uneasy night with shelling, etc. and in the early morning we moved up once more, a little further forward just below the plateau and were told to stay put because something big was going to be mounted to take Gemmano as it was such a tough nut.

It was a beautiful morning and comparatively quiet except for the odd bit of shelling. I was sitting down on an empty ammunition case, stripped to the waist, with my back resting against my tank writing up the Squadron War Diary and looking out over a wonderful vista because, as I have already said, the ground dropped away for something like 1500-2000 feet. Suddenly, once again without the slightest warning, there were three loud explosions all around me and I was simply covered in dust while stones and things were whizzing all over the place. The next moment, I don't remember doing it, I found myself about 20 feet away and up the mountainside, away from my tank, with my revolver out because I thought that a German patrol had got to the top of the mountain and had seen us and chucked down some hand-grenades. It was still very quiet and as the dust settled Shapcott poked his head out of the turret and started calling out, "Where are you Sir? Are you OK? Where are you?" and then he turned round and saw me. I put my hand up to my lips, telling him to shut-up and I indicated that he was to get out the tommy-gun and to go up the left side of me and that then the two of us would go to the top because I reckoned that the Jerries were up there. He understood and did that and I also indicated that the remainder of the crew should traverse the turret to point uphill to give us any covering fire that we might need. We laboriously and slowly crawled up and when we got to the top I felt an absolute damn fool because there was nothing up there at all. In fact, further along the spine of the ridge, we could see some of our infantry carrying out normal chores such as cleaning rifles and equipment, brewing up, smoking, etc. so, very puzzled, we walked back down to my tank again. I moved the ammunition box a few feet and carried on writing up the War Diary. I suppose about ten minutes later I heard the sound of laboured breathing and noise of stones and small rocks falling and thought, "Good grief! Someone is climbing up from the valley below." I quietly drew my revolver while Carter got hold of the tommy-gun, crouched down beside me and we both waited.

A hand appeared eventually over the edge of the track, then another, there was a heave and up came a British 'Battle Bowler' underneath which was the hot and sweating face of a very young, and I would think, a very new subaltern. He got to the edge of the track and stood up, taking a few moments to get his breath, during which time I said absolutely nothing at all but just looked at him. He looked a bit startled at my revolver and the tommy-gun and then, with an idiotic grin on his face, he came towards me holding out his hand and said, "Hello there! My name is so-and-so and I am with such-and-such a crowd down in the valley."

He then drew himself up rather proudly and said, "I am the Mortar Platoon Officer you know. I have just been firing my mortars for ranging and I wondered, by chance, if you had seen any land somewhere up here?" I regret to state that I jumped to my feet and grabbed him by his jacket and shook him and my language was absolutely ferocious because I said, "What the fucking hell did he think the fucking marks were on the track and what the fucking hell did he think had happened to my chest - which was covered in scratches and bits of sticking plaster and things - and if he was the Mortar Platoon Officer, before he fired his fucking mortars he ought to make sure it was fucking well clear where he was firing and not firing at one of his own fucking tanks." Carter came up and growled, "Shall I chuck the little bugger over the edge again Sir?" and I said to him, "Fucking good idea" and this silly idiot looked very alarmed and stepped backwards and said, "Steady on old boy there's no need for that" and nearly went over the edge and we had to grab him to stop him falling over.

*   *   *

It eventually took three proper co-ordinated attacks by infantry, artillery and tanks to take Gemmano, such was the German resistance, and I was damn pleased when we finally pulled out from this area as I thought my luck was beginning to run out.

The hoped-for breakthrough idea was completely off now of course and we were just being sucked into the general activities and as we were an independent Armoured Brigade and not attached to any one particular division we were therefore at the beck and call of any infantry crowd which wanted tank support - very similar to our role in the desert - and we were working with all sorts of units all over the place and three very odd things happened to me over the next couple of weeks or so whilst up in this mountainous country.

We were down in a valley somewhere, thankfully resting, when Peter got a message that one of the Queen's battalions was up on the top of a small mountain to our right and that they were being harried by accurate mortar and machine-gun fire. They were asking for tank fire support to counteract this so Peter told me to go up on a recce to see what help we could give them. I had to walk up for quite some way and found that the only route up to them was an exceptionally narrow mountain track with a steep bank to the left, about 15-20 feet high, and with the ground dropping away steeply to the immediate right down into another valley below. I doubted whether a tank could make it.

I got hold of my driver, Eric Mace, in place of L/Cpl. Clayton who was still away, and got him to walk up with me again and asked if he thought he could drive up there and he reckoned he could. However it was so narrow and dangerous that I made the rest of the crew dismount and walk up behind whilst I went up in front to direct him so that he wouldn't totter over the right hand edge. I suppose that it took the best part of 25-30 minutes to get to their BHQ with this method.

Once there the CO pointed out where the main trouble was coming from so we smartened up the Jerry positions with 75mm and machine-gun fire for some considerable time, moving around the mountain top and firing from different positions to give the enemy the impression there were more than one or two guns or tanks up there - to the huge delight of the CO and his men. By then it was nearly dark and he asked if I would stay with them for the rest of the night for moral support, etc. "Too true!" I replied, "I'm damned if I'm going down that track in the dark!" "Great!" he said, "You've certainly done your stuff alright and there will be no need to keep wireless watch as we are in touch with your Brigade - also there is no need to do any sentry duty as we will do that - so you can do what you like." This was simply wonderful news and I went back to my crew and told them that and they immediately started to prepare a meal. There seemed to be plenty of water up there, so I had some heated up and I stripped and had a wonderful wash all over, along with wolf whistles from my crew, especially when I had finished and put on a pair of rather snappy blue silk pyjamas which I had in my bed roll because I said if we were going to have a decent kip tonight I was going to do the job properly as I was fed up with sleeping in my bloody overalls and boots. The meal was good because somehow, somewhere, they had got hold of a chicken and some fresh vegetables and the odd bottle of wine and as soon as we had finished the meal we settled down to a really good nights sleep.

However, somewhere round about one or two o'clock in the morning, again it was a lovely warm night, things started up in earnest and we had to stand-to because a strong German fighting patrol got to within a 100 yards of us, but the infantry managed to beat them off and the CO came up to me and said, "I'm sorry about that but you won't get a lot of sleep in the next hour or two because we are mounting an attack ourselves and I have just given the order to my two companies down in the valley to start marching up and they will be marching right past you," and off he went.

I then realised that these wretched infantry were going to have to come up this long, long climb. It was dusty and it was warm and they were going to have to go over some very rotten terrain straight into an attack so I said to the crew, "Come on let's get the biggest brew going that we can to help these poor buggers." So we got a huge brew going and we laid out on the side of the tank provisions such as cheese, jam, bullybeef, spam, tinned fruit, cigarettes, etc. as we had plenty of stuff with us. We could hear the poor infantry plodding up this long, dusty hill whilst we waited for them.

The first man round the corner was their 'Point,' a corporal with his rifle and bayonet at the ready - they were doing the job properly - and I stepped forward and said, "Morning Corporal - care for some char?" He came to a full stop, looking at me blankly with his mouth open in utter astonishment and his bayonet damn nearly touching my chest and, without removing it or turning his head, he shouted out, "Hey Sarge! There's a fooking tank up 'ere," and back came the reply, anxiously, "What is it? One of theirs or one of ours?" "It's a fooking Sherman ain't it." "Well, that's alright then." "What's more there's a fooking bloke - in fooking 'jamas - dishin' out fooking cups of fooking char!" Back came the reply, "Are you off your flaming rocker Ginger?" "Well, if you don't fooking believe me come and have a fooking look yerself." Back came a final reply, "I bloody well will and don't you move!"

The sergeant must have thought that his corporal had flipped his lid because he cautiously came around the corner, a tough looking bloke with his Sten gun at the ready, so I carefully pushed the rifle and bayonet away from my chest because the corporal was still standing in shock, looking at me, and said to the Sergeant, with a grin on my face, "You know your Corporal is perfectly right. Perhaps you would like some char?" as I offered him a mug of hot tea.

He took a couple of steps backward, pushing his helmet off his forehead and said, "Bloody 'ell Sir! What the 'ell's going on?!" As I suppose he hardly expected to see a chap in pyjamas, smoking a pipe and dishing out mugs of tea off the side of a tank on a mountain top, under these circumstances and at this ungodly hour of the morning.

You can imagine the comments of the infantry chaps as they came past my tank and crew who were dishing out the goodies etc. "Cor! fucking Tankies: What a fucking way to go to a fucking war! Hey, Bert! What about a transfer to the fucking Tank Corps? No bloody fear mate! They brew-up too fucking easy!" and so on. Of course my crew were giving back tit-for-tat: "you need to be fucking intelligent to be in Tanks mate," ... "fucking daft you mean Tankie" etc. It was wonderful to hear this repartee.

One of their company commanders came up to me with his mug of tea and asked if it was my idea and when I said that it was he hit me so hard on the back that I nearly fell over and just about scalded my feet with my hot tea. He then said, "If it's the last thing I ever bloody well do I'll see that you get a mention in our Battalion War Diary for this. Thanks! A terrific effort," and off they went into their attack.

It was well worth it and I hope that there is a short note in their War Diary to the effect that, "...on such-and-such a date a successful night attack was carried out at such-and-such a place - aided and abetted by 'a certain tank and crew of 8th RTR.'"

*   *   *

A day or so later we were up on the top of another blasted ridge having laboriously pushed the Jerry forces back at some cost to ourselves. As usual, we had no support with us and were being absolutely stonked to blazes, being plastered with all kinds of nastiness and it was virtually impossible to get out of the tank because the concentrations were so prolonged and fierce. However, the combination of this and the fact that I had been eating rather a lot of grapes meant that I had very definitely to go outside to pay a very urgent call of nature.

I told my crew what as soon as it was a bit quiet I was going to do and said, "For God's sake don't move because I will be squatting beside, or even underneath, the tank." They said, "OK Sir but get a ruddy move on." When it did eventually quieten down a little I clambered out, stood on the side and jumped and, as I hit the ground, it gave way beneath me. There was the most appalling, disgusting smell that I have ever smelt in my life and I was immediately covered with hordes of the foulest and most filthy flies of every possible description as I sank up to my knees in the rotting carcass of a cow. It was absolutely obscene, the filth, the slime, the grubs and flies, everything and with a scream of horror I jumped out and, rather like a demented dervish, I was running around trying to swat the flies and at the same time cleaning myself down with handfuls of grass, etc. I was observed of course and down came a damned stonk again all around me, so I had to fling myself flat on my face alongside this filthy, stinking corruption. In the end I couldn't endure it any longer and hastily scrambled back inside my tank.

Of course, when I did that, the crew held their noses and said, "Christ! What have you done Sir!" and they cut off my overall trousers, above the knees, with the help of the first-aid scissors and I had to throw them out of the turret and then tried to clean my boots and socks as best I could.

The 'B' Echelon was unable to get up to us for about a day and a half so, for that period of time, I was going about looking like a hillbilly character with these ragged trousers. When a radio message went back that evening that, "Captain Hamilton needs a pair of overall trousers, boots and clean socks urgently" - well - it gave rise to all sorts of rumours back at the Echelon as to what exactly I had been doing to myself.

By now it was coming up to mid-September - the weather being absolutely glorious with long, warm days of unbroken sunshine - but it was a long, hard, slogging match because we were having to do this dual job of tanks and infantry. We would come up against the inevitable ridge or crest, blast away at it with 75mm and machine-gun fire, crawl down into the bottom of the valley, and then tortuously work our way up the top only to find that the damned Jerries had retired back to the next crest, so that we would have to do it all over again - and again - and again. It was all very exhausting and frustrating having no infantry with us.

On September 14th an absolute and totally unnecessary tragedy happened and, even now, after all these years, it makes me so mad. We had gradually pushed ourselves up over a ridge and then down into a valley and were under intensive and concentrated shell-fire but, somehow or other, we had managed to get about two Troops onto the forward crest, but that was all, as the stonking was so fierce and heavy.

We had lost several tanks by then and I had managed to get forward on foot and found the crews, who had gathered in one or two small outbuildings: a couple were stretcher cases and two or three suffering from burns. I got back again and we radioed for the Recce Troop to come forward to pick them up. This they did with two of their Honey half-tracks, i.e. Honey tanks with the turret removed. They came down the rear slope towards us and it was simply incredible the way they were stonked all the way down but fortunately not hit and they carried on to where the wounded were lying. They picked them all up, laying the two stretcher cases across the back, and slowly went back up the reverse slope once more. This time, however, the Jerries remarkably did not fire a single shot as one of the Honey crew had hoisted a Red Cross flag and the Jerries decently and correctly observed the Geneva Convention to the full.

This was the position for the rest of the day, almost until it was dark, when Peter Butt was then told on the radio that he was required to go back and report to Big Sunray, i.e. our Brigadier 'PP.'

When Peter got angry his face used to go white and his mouth would twitch and when he eventually came back he looked like a ghost and his face was like a gargoyle. He was absolutely livid and I had never seen him so angry and furious as this.

He came up to me and said, almost choking, that the bloody Brigadier 'PP' had told him that he - Peter - was incompetent and a coward, his Squadron was useless and that though we were going to be relieved by the 2nd RTR, as a punishment (!) he was ordering Peter to go forward on a recce because once the 2nd RTR had come up and taken over from us they were then going to push on, in strength, to the top of the ridge and beyond. I simply could not believe this and could well understand his anger and I was hopping mad, myself, at this completely unfair and slanderous attack on Peter and the Squadron. As the 2nd RTR were going to do an attack immediately on taking over from us it was obviously their job to do the necessary recce and if it was anyone's job in 'B' Squadron to do a recce then it was mine and not Peter's.

However, he went out that night with a small recce party but unfortunately they were observed and heavily shelled and Peter and Sgt. Beavers were killed and two or three others wounded. It was an absolutely unnecessary tragedy with the loss of a super bloke, a very fine and very popular officer - and a good friend - I can never, ever forgive 'PP' for that murderous and simply criminal order. RSM Parry and I attended his simple funeral.

I then had to take over the Squadron under these very unfortunate circumstances and, once again, rather a bizarre incident happened to me. We had pushed forward and, as usual, were lining a ridge but everything that particular morning seemed to be unnaturally and beautifully quiet. It was another glorious day with brilliant sunshine, birds singing, etc., so I managed to walk up to the forward Troops to see that everything was OK and then dropped down into the valley on my way back to my Squadron HQ. I was feeling very happy and contented with life, found a convenient large bush, lit my pipe and squatted down to do my 'morning glory.' When I had finished and was pulling up my trousers and buckling on my revolver belt, to my complete astonishment a large bush which was only some five yards or so away from me moved and parted and - out stepped a German soldier. Quite instinctively, and before one could say 'Jack Robinson,' my pistol was out and pointing at him and I was absolutely petrified thinking, "Good God Almighty! What's happening? Has a Jerry patrol got round behind us? If so where the hell's the rest of them?" I then looked at him properly and saw, first of all, that he was very young, he couldn't have been more than 17, if that: he was ashen-faced with sweat pouring off his face, dripping down his chin and dropping onto the dusty track. His face was covered in a sort of ginger 'bum-fluff,' he was that young, and he was unarmed as his shaking hands were level with his shoulders. My intense fright turned to intense anger and rage as I realised that this fucking little so-and-so had been watching me do something very intimate and personal and my finger curled on the trigger. His eyes were almost popping out of his head because he could see the emotions on my face as he really thought that he was going to be shot and By God! I nearly shot him there and then. But, thank God! my rage subsided and my sanity returned and I stepped back and lowered my pistol.

When I did that he just sank down onto his knees, putting his face in his hands, half-pushing his coal-scuttle helmet off, and burst into completely hysterical and uncontrollable sobbing. So much so that I holstered my pistol, walked up to him and put my arms around his shoulders, murmuring idiotically, "OK, OK, Tedschi OK, La guerra finita per voi. You're alright old boy, stop crying." I then walked him back, still with my arm around him as he was shaking and sobbing, to my SHQ which was a small farmhouse nestling in the lee of the valley. I felt like an old man comforting a young child.

When I arrived the men came up to me and gathered round, looking curious, and saying. "Bloody 'ell Sir! What 'ave you got there! Where did you find it! etc. etc." They crowded round the poor little blighter and with the typical sympathy of the English soldier someone eventually said, "Hey! Come on Fritz! Have a fag - get the poor little sod a cuppa!" and that is the last I ever saw or heard of that German soldier. I have often thought of that incident since then and I wonder today if there is, somewhere in Germany, a slightly balding, ginger haired, portly, retired businessman walking around and wonder what sort of story he recounts of his fighting in the Gothic Line - whether he fought courageously to the last round before he was overwhelmed, or when he deserted and gave himself up he was very nearly shot but was saved by the compassion of a British officer who had seen quite enough unnecessary killing by then. However, it was a very, very close thing and he was never so near to death as he was at that moment but, once again, thank God I didn't pull the trigger.

It would seem that I would be pushing my luck if I stated that another bizarre incident happened in this area at around that time, but it did. It was the usual situation, we had been pushing forward without any support, and I had managed to get two Troops onto a ridge but the rest of us were further back in a valley and it was simply impossible to go forward to help them owing to the tremendously heavy shelling and the fact that we had very few tanks left. Robbie was in charge of the two troops and said they seemed to be OK up there so long as they kept quiet. There were some infantry up there of ours, dug-in, and it was just the shelling going on behind the ridge stopping any reinforcements coming up, and he would call for help if it was necessary.

Previously I had radioed back and said we wanted some supplies of petrol and ammunition because we were getting a bit low, and miraculously two or three lorries managed to come up to where I was with these supplies and one of the drivers had brought a sack of mail with him, which was a marvellous tonic for all of us. As things had quietened down a bit by then I decided I would go up on foot to where Robbie and the Troops were and take the mail as I felt they would appreciate that. On the way I came across a deserted farm which was still smouldering as it had been hit earlier that morning and there were quite a few bodies around, which was rather unpleasant, and on the far side of it, i.e. closer to the Jerry positions, was a knocked-out Sherman. It wasn't one of ours and I approached rather cautiously because there had been stories that the Jerries, when retreating, were apt to booby-trap such vehicles as this. I carefully looked around it but couldn't see anything suspicious and clambered up onto the turret to have a look inside. It had been penetrated and set on fire and was pretty nasty inside with the usual hoard of flies and unpleasant smell. I was observed doing this and down came the whistle and scream of a salvo of shells which crashed all about me in the farmyard and I almost pressed myself through the armour of the turret in my fright. As I did that I suddenly felt something wet and sticky going down my left thigh and I thought, "Oh my God! I've been hit" and gingerly felt it with my hand. It was horribly sticky and when the stonk finished I looked down and saw that my overalls were messy, then looked at my hand - smelt it and thought, "That's funny, that's not blood" and then I thought, "Oh! No..."

I said that I had been walking around a farm and just before getting up onto the tank I'd picked up three eggs and put them in my overall pocket and in my fright, when I had pressed myself so hard against the turret, I'd smashed all the ruddy eggs.

So, once again, a message was passed back down to 'B' Echelon that Major Hamilton wanted another pair of overall trousers and shorts. I really was getting a stinking reputation back in 'B' Echelon! We were then right into the very heart of the Gothic Line defences in this terrible mountain country which was totally unsuitable for tanks, but the 8th Army had by then had heavy casualties in infantry and the assault troops were very tired - as indeed we all were - and we, the tanks, were having to do this dual role of continuously probing forward without any artillery or infantry support at all and trying to capture ground and hold it, which was totally against all proper tank tactics. A determined German infantry battalion could quite easily hold up an entire infantry brigade of ours - which indeed they were doing - because the terrain was so suitable for defence and so impossible for attack. We were then in the region of Coriano, another of these interminable mountain ridges, somewhat north and east of Monte Gemmano. We had carried out an attack in the morning, probing up forward, and had got up pretty well to the top of the crest but once again very heavy concentrations of shell, mortar and anti-tank fire were holding us up - we had had many casualties by then and unfortunately one of our replacement officers, a Captain Tim Newman ex-lst Army was killed, his tank being hit and set on fire, this being his first action with us, and one of our old hands Sergeant Nunnington was hit and set on fire and badly burnt and, as far as I can remember, the total regimental strength was only about 14 or 15 tanks of which my Squadron contributed about five.

I had gone up on foot with Corporal Adams (MM and Bar) of 'C' Squadron because I had observed some movement around some sort of odd out-buildings or dug-outs and we both went up with tommy-guns to see what the situation was, and recce the ground to find out whether the tanks could get up any further, but it was far too steep. The dug-outs were empty except for three or four wounded tank crew, with a couple suffering from burns, so once again we radioed for the Recce Troop to come up and help get them out and also asked for some support.

I was talking to Sunray (our CO) about this on the radio when to my surprise another voice came on the air and asked, "Would it help if 'Big Sunray Brown Jobs' (the infantry brigadier) came up for a look at the situation?" Before I had time to press my microphone to reply an unknown operator came on the air and said, "It would be a fucking good idea mate!"

I little later I walked down the hill to the bottom of the valley with Tom Hendrie DSO ('A' Squadron OC) and to our disgust we found that our CO had come up in his tank, closed down, and had put it into a ditch on its side and he was lying in a fold of the ground with his tin hat on. His nerve had completely gone and his arms and hands were covering his face and head and he was jerking and shuddering at every shell burst that came near. The infantry brigadier, who had come up with him, was looking pretty upset at this. Tom and I gave our reports and I confirmed that I had been up some way on foot to see what the ground was like but that it was impossible for tanks to get up any further; that we had no infantry support whatsoever; that there were wounded men about and that we would need infantry and, in particular, artillery support preferably with plenty of smoke to cover us from the severe anti-tank gun fire from our exposed right flank.

Anyway, we were very low on ammunition and petrol, as well as being very few in numbers as we could barely muster a dozen, if that, several of which had been hit and were hardly in a fit state to be classified as runners. The infantry brigadier said that he hadn't realised the situation was as bad as it was and he would do his utmost to get something done about it as soon as he could. We had to stay up there until it was pretty well dark and then we pulled back down into the valley for supplies, etc. and whilst we were down there we came under extremely heavy stonking which was very, very accurate. We tried to move around a bit but wherever we went it followed us. Suddenly there was a shout from, I think, Reggie Hooper, our Recce Troop captain as he discovered a German artillery observation officer who was in a well camouflaged dug-out and this blighter was directing this heavy fire right onto us. He was very quickly dealt with, though he was a brave man to do what he had been doing.

On the morning of September 18th yet another dawn attack on yet another blasted ridge, The Cerasolo Ridge, which was just about the last one defending the town of Rimini on the edge of the Lombardi Plain - this had been the original objective early on about September 8th/9th.

We moved up very slowly, again without any artillery or infantry support, and we could only muster about nine or ten tanks in the Regiment. By the time dawn was breaking we were probably about two-thirds of the way up the ridge and it was getting steeper and steeper the more we went forward. Jerry suddenly became aware of what was happening and of course down came the inevitable stonking. For some unknown reason I was the extreme outside right-hand tank and as the dawn was breaking I could see the valley stretching away for miles down to my right and could even see a glimmer of the sea because we were only about ten miles or so inland.

The ground to our left was completely impossible for tanks as it was so steep and rocky. We just couldn't move up any further and away down in the valley down on my right were probably at least 20 knocked-out tanks, some of them being ours which we had lost a day or so before, also tanks from other units and it looked a pretty desperate situation and I was extremely uneasy about this open right flank.

I was reporting back on the wireless to Sunray about this, stating that we were very small in numbers and that we were completely exposed for miles on the right and that we would require a very much bigger force to help take this ridge, with concentrations of smoke to cover this right flank when, somehow, our own Big Sunray, (this infernal 'PP') got on the air. He was shouting incomprehensible orders stating, "There's a fox on the loose - there's a fox on the run - go after him - get him, get him." I then suddenly saw a flash way over to my right on the ridge and, to my horror, I saw red tracer simply streaking towards me. I was absolutely paralysed with fright because I knew what it was and with a whoosh! like an express train a 75mm or 88mm screamed past my head and slammed straight into my sergeant's tank next to me which immediately burst into flames. Desperately trying to sound calm I ordered my driver to reverse left as fast as he could and my gunner to traverse right and to my tortured mind it seemed ages before either of them responded, but this was not so because they were a damn good crew and their reactions were almost instantaneous. Just as we started to move I again saw another flash and, once more, red tracer streaking towards me and I was saying to myself, "Oh God! please no no!" and the shell was so close to the left side of my head that I swear I felt the heat of it as it screamed past and slammed into my third tank, another sergeant, which also went straight up in flames.

My gunner had seen the flash and immediately put down three or four HE shells with very accurate shooting and Robbie, who was the only tank left in the Squadron with me, just two of us out of 16, also joined in firing at the ridge and between the two of us we blasted away for probably five or six minutes. We now only mustered about nine tanks in the Regiment out of 52 and the others pulled back very slightly to try and get some sort of cover and in spite of the smoke and the unpleasant smell I manoeuvred my own in between the two burning Shermans as this gave me some sort of protection. As I have mentioned earlier the reason why the Sherman brewed-up so quickly was that the armour was only about two-and-a-half inches thick, which was hopelessly thin by then, and any German anti-tank gun could easily penetrate this. We were sitting on 90 gallons of high octane fuel and in the turret we carried about 100 rounds of 75mm ammo. Most of which was high-explosive: up to 5,000 rounds of .30 Browning machine-gun ammunition and several dozen mortar bombs. Penetration invariably caused an explosion, followed by fire, and the Jerries had an unpleasant but accurate nickname for Shermans, calling them "Tommy Cookers." We were still being very heavily stonked as well with all sorts of fire, 75's, 105's, 88 air bursts, Nebelwerfers, the whole damn lot because this really was the last ridge in the Gothic Line defences immediately in front of Rimini. In fact I could just see the edge of the town around the crest of the hill as Jerry was slinging everything at us to prevent the breakthrough whilst they were preparing to evacuate the place and move back along Route 9 up the Lombardi Plain back towards Bologna.

I reported back on the wireless once more and thank God this time I didn't speak to Big Sunray but to someone with more sense who seemed to understand the situation and he shortly came up on the air and said we were to hold on and were being relieved later that morning. By mid-afternoon I asked what had happened and the message was that we were still to hang on and that relief was on the way and we were to stay and they would take over by the time it was dark. This didn't happen and when it was dark we pulled back down to the bottom of the hill into the valley to leaguer. We were all desperately tired by then and we still had to mount guard and everything of course because we had no infantry to do this job for us. In order to keep myself awake and be sure that everything was all right I continuously prowled round the perimeter of this small group of us to make sure that everybody was doing the job properly. I was also on the air two or three times during the night asking when the relief would be arriving and, once again, was told they would be up at about first light. We stood to as usual at dawn so wearily I gave the order to start moving up the hill once more and thought, "Here we go again..." When suddenly there was the most marvellous sound and sight as about 30

Shermans, I suppose two Squadrons, of the Queen's Bays appeared down in the valley on our right. As soon as they saw our little group up the hill, to my utter dismay, they all started to swing left so that their guns were facing towards us and they appeared to be taking no defensive action on their dangerous right flank - this which I had continuously stressed in every wireless message I had passed back. I told my wireless-operator to get on immediately to RHQ and to pass on this information also to try and find out the Bays wireless wavelength to warn them as I jumped out and started running towards them. Their nearest tank was, I suppose, about 300-400 yards away and I was running as fast as I could over very difficult sloping, rocky ground. I was shouting, which of course was useless, and waving and pointing my arms over to the right and one or two of their tank commanders saw me and started waving back. I knew what was going to happen and to my horror before I was able to reach them there was 'Bang! Bang!' and two of their Shermans went up in flames. I climbed wearily onto their first tank which was commanded by a young, white-faced, second lieutenant and he looked at me in horror and said, "Christ! What's happening up here?" and I said, "haven't you been warned about that flank?" and he answered, "What flank?" so I said, "Where's your Squadron Commander?" and he pointed him out to me and, again this chap was about a further 200-300 yards away so I ran across and jumped up onto the back of his tank. This time he was a fine and handsome looking young man wearing a cavalry fore and aft hat, clean and freshly shaved, whereas I must have looked an absolute scruff as I hadn't washed or shaved for about two or three days and my face was still puffy and I had the remains of a black eye where I had been hit on the cheek a few days earlier by a shell splinter and I was very, very tired indeed.

   He looked at me and then down at the knocked-out tanks down in the valley and asked, "Are those yours down there?" "Most of them" I replied. He then gestured to the little group of us up on the hill and asked, "Is that your Squadron up there?" "No" I replied grimly, "That's what's left of the Regiment." "Good God!" he exclaimed, "You must have had a real pasting!"

   I then asked him if he hadn't been warned about the anti-tank guns on the exposed right flank and he replied, "No, not at all" and I just couldn't believe this. He said that all they had been told was to take over the position from us. Whilst we were talking there was, 'Bang!'

'Bang!' 'Bang!', three more shots and three more Shermans in flames. It was incredibly good shooting but devastating to watch and comprehend. He then told me to hang on and rapidly gave some orders on the air and the Squadrons started to re-deploy and face out to the threat. I then briefed him further as much as I could and he nodded and said, "OK thanks. Off you go as we will take over now."

We then re-grouped and pulled back some three or four miles to a rest area and our acting CO, Major Peter Hordern OBE, gave the order that all the 'Echelon' and spare crews were to refuel and re-ammo the tanks and that the tank crews that had just come back were to do nothing at all but rest as he could see that by then we were all completely and utterly exhausted.

I had a quick check to see that everyone left in 'B' Squadron was OK and then just crashed out to sleep. This was fairly early evening and it seemed to me only a few minutes later, though it must have been some three to four hours because by then it was dark, that I slowly started to wake up, irritatedly feeling that something was tickling the back of my neck and down my spine and I could also hear an unusual noise, a sort of hissing sound. I then woke up with a jerk to find that it was raining heavily and as I was lying in some sort of gully on the side of the hill that the damn water was coming down the back of my neck, down my back and out through my trousers. It was a cruel irony of fate that the weather, which had been glorious, warm and fine should have broken at the precise moment when all we wanted to do was sleep.

I think that I was too tired even to curse and we all climbed wearily into the tank. The driver, co-driver and gunner on to their seats, Carter curling up on the floor and I slumped onto my Tank Commander's seat, draped over the gun, and spent the rest of the night like that in sopping wet clothes.

We were back fairly quickly once more, about September 28th, in the area of Savignano and we were then working with another crowd, the 4/10th Baluchis of the 4th Indian Division, old desert comrades. The weather had cleared momentarily and that evening I was at the headquarters of the Indian infantry battalion situated in a small farmhouse nestling in the valley of a small crest, liaising with them for a forthcoming attack. Their CO suggested that I should spend the night there as they would have further information from fighting patrols that were going out that night. We could then get down to it properly the next day and he invited me to bed down in the farmhouse with them.

However, it was full of jabbering Indians, with two or three wireless sets going, and awful smells of various curries being cooked so I said that I would sleep outside beside my Honey tank in the courtyard. The CO said, "You had better be careful because we get quite a bit of stonking here you know" and left me to my own devices.

I went out and told the crew this gen and the three of them got underneath the Honey and I set up my rickety old camp bed alongside the tank and dropped off to a very welcome, deep sleep.

Somewhere around about midnight I was awakened very abruptly.

I was lying flat on my back, looking up at a wonderful deep blue sky which was ablaze with stars, but coming out of the heavens straight towards me were five flaming meteors making the most awful screaming, moaning sound. They were five six-inch mortar rockets from a Nebelwerfer and they were coming right at me.

I was just paralysed with sheer fright and terror, unable to move, and just pressing myself down in my bed as hard as I could. There was the most tremendous explosion and crash as they hit the farmhouse and courtyard all around me, and at the precise moment they exploded on impact, such was my fright, I burst all the rotten old straps and canvas and the bed and wooden legs collapsed and enfolded me so I was thrashing about like a trussed chicken absolutely swearing my head off.

The crew were helpless with laughter at my dilemma and said that they had never heard such swear words and language and didn't know half the ones that I was using. Unfortunately the Nebelwerfer set fire to the roof of the farmhouse and killed three or four chaps and wounded another half-a-dozen and it also set fire to two lorries and I am afraid I spent the rest of the night underneath the tank with the rest of the crew.

On October 7th we were then preparing to help the infantry get across the river Fiumchino which was just north of Savignano. Here a most rotten stupid accident happened. Corporal Clayton, my driver who had been slightly wounded in the face at Monte Gemmano, came back to us. It was fairly late in the afternoon when he came up and said he was quite ready to drive my tank again. I told him that as he hadn't been briefed he couldn't come into this operation but he could join us the next morning. He was a bit upset about this but understood the reason and wandered off to speak to two or three of his friends. I then started walking round the Squadron warning them to be prepared to move off in about half-an-hour's time. I saw Corporal Clayton sitting on some blankets with his back to a tank reading the 8th Army News with a cigarette drooping from his mouth and his beret on the back of his head and the driver of this particular tank came up and said, "Get off my blankets Tim you lazy bugger." He pulled at the blankets and a shot rang out and Clayton looked startled and fell over sideways with blood trickling from the side of his mouth. I ran up to him and as I picked him up in my arms he just gasped, "Oh Sir" and died.

What had happened was that in the blankets, for some unknown reason, was a revolver and the effect of the driver pulling them either cocked it and fired it or it was cocked and it fired and the bullet went through Clayton's lower stomach and came out through his heart. It was a complete accident and a very cruel trick of fate that a fine young chap, he was only 23, should have to die under these circumstances after all he had been through. He was a damn fine driver, steady as a rock in action and very much liked by the rest of the Squadron and of course I reported him as a proper battle casualty.

In 1968 my wife and I were on holiday in Italy and we stayed just south of Rimini, in the Cattolica area, and it was most evocative and extraordinary touring round the old Gothic Line battle area.

Fortunately my wife, bless her, had always taken a very keen interest in the Regiment and what it did during the War and at various reunions she was able to talk not only about the different battles, both in the Desert and Italy, but even of the individuals who had taken part. So much so that Hickey Sugden said that she knew as much, if not more, than those who had taken part. We had taken the car into the mountains and it was extraordinary for me to be there once again, with such memories, and to point out to her where various incidents had occurred - and she knew and understood. To my surprise we came across a beautiful little cemetery on the outskirts of Coriano, where we had such a bitter battle, and I had had no idea it was there.

It was a beautiful afternoon in late May and the countryside was looking at its very best. The cemetery was deserted and we were quite on our own as we wandered around for about an hour or more. It was beautifully kept with the grasses cleanly cut, trim verges, fresh flowers on many of the graves and no litter. Unfortunately I could not find any 8th RTR graves but I saw many of the other Tank Regiments, particularly the Queen's Bays, also several infantry units we had worked with in that battle.

My wife was in tears at some of the inscriptions, particularly at the young ages and one moved me greatly. It was for Pte. Johnny Xthantopolis - age 17 - Princess Patricia's Canadian Light Infantry and the headstone simply said, "He Came From Mexico." Just what a young Mexican boy was doing in a Canadian outfit, under British Command, fighting Germans in Italy - well - it made me think...

As we were leaving my wife turned round for one more look, and I am quite convinced that she was meant to do just that, as she suddenly grabbed my arm tightly and said, "Darling! Look," she was pointing to a grave to my right one row away and the headstone said:

TO THE MEMORY OF LANCE CORPORAL T. CLAYTON; AGE 23; 'B' SQUADRON 8TH RTR; RIP.

My driver who had died in my arms in October 1944 (almost as if, out of those thousands of graves there, he had lifted his arm and said, "Here I am Sir").

*   *   *

A few days later I was up at the infantry Brigade Headquarters as the Squadron was going to be used in close support of the infantry getting across the river Rubicon. This time the Squadron was going to be in close support in the village itself whilst the Infantry went across the river and secured a beach-head and cleared it of mines before we went across ourselves. I wanted to do a recce myself before anything started and it was suggested that I went out that night with an RE officer and a fighting patrol of three or four infantry so I could have a look at the village and the positions the tanks would take up. The RE officer was an amazing bloke, he had actually been in tanks at one time but had transferred to the REs, (God knows why!) and he said he had been across the river and it was very low still because the rains hadn't properly started, and volunteered to come up and show me exactly where we would have to cross.

It was fairly quiet up in that area with only spasmodic shell fire and machine-gun fire - probably firing on fixed lines - but as it was at night it seemed that everybody was firing directly at ourselves and the infantry patrol just disappeared and left the RE bloke and myself on our 'Jack Jones.' We got up to the river and I could see it was only a couple of feet deep, if that, at the ford area, and he said he had been across the other side for about a hundred yards or more and would I like to go across as well, to which I replied, "No fear!" I had come up quite far enough because we weren't going to go across until the infantry had actually made sure it was absolutely clear of mines, so we turned round and started to walk back. Previously there had been strong moonlight, which made it seem rather eerie, but a lot of heavy cloud had come up by now which obscured the moon and for some unknown reason we started to talk in whispers as we walked back through the deserted village.

I then suddenly grabbed his arm, told him to stop talking, saying, "Did you hear that?" and then again I heard a curious sort of stumbling, shuffling noise coming down the dusty track towards us. We both stopped and he whispered, "What the hell's that?" I whispered back that I thought it might be a Jerry patrol and that they had a wounded man with them as this shuffling sound stopped every now and then as if they were dragging him along. The RE officer had no revolver or anything with him and I just had my revolver and two hand grenades so I gave him one and whispered that he should go into the ditch on one side of the track and that I would drop back a few paces into the ditch on the other side. I said, "For Christ's sake don't throw the grenade back towards me if you have to throw it at all." We both got into position and waited nervously and I had my grenade in my left hand, with the pin slightly loosened, and my revolver in my right hand ready for almost anything. After what seemed an age the shuffling started coming towards us again and there was a tremendous Bang! and a flash almost immediately in front of me as the RE chap threw his grenade. This was followed by a huge bellow of fright and anger and something big, dark, hairy and smelly crashed into me, knocking me flat on my back as I fired my pistol into the air, but Thank God! I kept the grenade in my hand as a damned cow went bellowing up the road at full gallop. Incidentally, this was the only time I fired my revolver during the entire war.

When we got back to the infantry Brigade Headquarters and I was reporting to the Brigade Major and laughingly telling him this, he looked at me rather curiously and said, "Where did you say this happened?" and I pointed out on the map where the track was and he said, "Good heavens this map in hopelessly out of date, when did you get it?" I said, "A couple of days ago" and he said, "Where you have been walking, on the latest maps, the area is shown to be very heavily mined, full of these German 'S' mines all along the ditches and hedgerows, exactly where you have been." I think that was very definitely a case of 'ignorance is bliss!'

With the fall of Rimini on September 21st, one day after the Regiment had been pulled back, the Gothic Line had finally been broken and it had taken the 8th Army some 26 days to advance a mere 30 miles owing to the impossible territory over which we had been operating and a very determined and stubborn resistance by the German forces.

The 8th Army had suffered over 14,000 casualties during this period, approximately 540 infantry a day, and about 300 tanks had been destroyed which was the equivalent of nearly a squadron a day and General Alexander reported, "Tanks were easily replaceable but the men were not." During this period the 8th Army took over 8,000 German prisoners and I believe that their total casualties during this period, including killed, wounded and missing, had been in excess of 20,000 so this shows how very bitter and bloody was the Gothic Line battle.

The casualties the 8th RTR suffered in the three weeks of active fighting in the Gothic Line totalled some 120, consisting of 22 officers and 98 other ranks. This represented 50% of the tank crew force and it was approximately the loss of over one tank crew (five men) per day for this period.

Further casualties occurred in the winter fighting and up to the end of the War in Italy on May 2nd 1945 but fortunately not on this scale.In the Western Desert campaigns of 1941-1942 the casualties totalled some 140-150. This consisted of about 26-28 officers and 118-126 other ranks.

These figures may seem rather small compared with the heavy losses in infantry battalions, or in the Royal Navy and Merchant Navy when whole ship's companies were lost; or in the Royal Air Force, particularly Bomber Command, with eight to ten men per aircraft. However in the Desert in Valentine tanks we had three-man crews, so in a Regimental strength of 52 tanks this meant there were 156 tank crews so that losses of 140-150 over a 13 month period were, comparatively speaking, pretty severe. Again, in Italy, we had Sherman tanks with five-man crews, so in a Regimental strength, again of 52 tanks, this meant a total of 260 tank crews. Thus, 120 casualties in just a three week period shows losses of nearly 50%.

Naturally the 'A' and 'B' Echelons also suffered losses but on nothing like the scale of the tank crews. The total casualties of the 8th RTR in the Desert and Italian campaigns were approximately 280/300. Some 123 were killed, ie nearly 45%.

General Alexander subsequently reported that to carry on with the attack to push the Germans right back into the Alps he needed a superiority of at least three to one, but he never had anything like this at all and it was doubtful if at this particular stage of the campaign the superiority was as much as two to one, because so many men had been sent back to England for the D-Day landings in France.

Having fought through incredibly difficult mountain country we now came up against a completely different terrain altogether and I now quote from *The Gothic Line* by Douglas Orgill. This is a splendid book.

> The Lombardi plain as a terrain for an armoured breakthrough was soon to be proved an Army mirage. 8th Army was now entering the Romagna on the south east corner of the plain and the Romagna could hardly have been more effective anti-tank country if it had been artificially constructed for the purpose. 8th Army was now out of the hills. Now it faced the rivers.

> Water was now the main obstacle for the Army's advance rather than high ground, General Alexander reported later. The whole area is nothing but a reclaimed swamp - and not wholly reclaimed in some parts - formed by the lower courses of the numerous rivers flowing down from the Appenines in their new north easterly direction. The principal rivers are, in order from south to north, the Uso, the Savio, the Ronco, the Montone, the Lamone, the Senio, the Santerno, the Sillaro and the Idice; these are only the principal rivers and there are hundreds of smaller streams, canals and irrigation ditches between them. Even in the best plain areas the soil remembers its marshy origin and when rained on forms the richest mud known to the Italian theatre. It will be seen that under Autumn conditions we should have difficulty in making full use of our armoured superiority.

> It rained very heavily on the night of the 20th and the rain continued with heavy drizzle and drenching showers intermittently until the 29th when the skies opened and a violent rain storm continued for four days.

> The brown torrents of the growing river surged down the stony beds of summer; bridges and roads disappeared; the infantry and armour floundered in a desolate sea of mud. Each of the hundreds of farmhouses, flood banks, lines of vines which spread out across the Romagna could house a German Spandau machine-gun or 88 millimetre gun; the ground was cultivated in neat little olive groves and orchards which made excellent battle positions and the first that the Allied

Infantry could know about a post was when the Spandau suddenly cut into them from a flank or the 88 opened fire. The north Italian plain had been overestimated from the start by the 8th Army planners as a suitable terrain for a swift advance. Even in the dust and heat of summer the area would have inhibited the Allied advance by reasons of the local agricultural methods alone; under Autumn and Winter conditions it was passable only by a long slogging advance which would cost many men, weeks and months of time.

Not only did this terrain operate against the 8th Army's rapid advance but there were two other factors as well. The first was that the German retreat was not disorganised in any way. It was a very carefully controlled and a very stubborn and bitter resistance put up by them all the way back up to Bologna, which was approximately 60 miles north, and utilizing every obstacle and difficulty of ground to their full advantage. The second factor was that the rains came early that year by about two weeks and that completely bogged us down so that we had to spend another winter before driving the enemy out of Italy, slowly and painfully inching our way forward through this very difficult terrain.

Round about the period October 11th-14th we completely pulled out and went back to Porto Recanate, a delightful little town right on the Adriatic coast and it was wonderful having a complete break and rest from action and being able to get full sleep, proper meals, leave etc. We were reinforced with men back up to our full strength and picked up fresh tanks and after about four or five weeks we then moved up into the area round about Forlimpopoli, which was about five or six miles south and east of Forli on Route 9. The Squadron was billeted in various small farmhouses scattered around the area and one day Sergeant Tony Talbot, one of my Troop Sergeants, approached me and asked to have a private conversation. He was a real character, having been a regular soldier and served out in India before the war, and as the Sergeant-Major dourly remarked, "He ought to have the nickname Yo-Yo," because he had been up and down from sergeant to private and back again so many times that it was difficult to keep track of his progress in the army. He was a splendid man to have in action, completely reliable then, but what a headache when he was behind the lines. Somehow he had got hold of an extraordinary black leather hat, rather like an engine driver's hat, and he also sported rather long black sideburns and again the Sergeant-Major grimly remarked, on more than one occasion, "Sergeant Talbot, I'll have those bloody sideburns off you when we are out of the line, if not I'll have your stripes as well, that is if you've got any left by then."

He told me he had a request to make and would I hear his story before I made any comment, and asked if he could have a three-ton lorry for one afternoon during the next day or so because it was a very urgent matter. It was extremely difficult then to authorise transport other than on direct army requirements. He went on to explain that in no way did he want to use it for blackmarket (!) reasons, i.e. the flogging of petrol, rations, etc., but that it was for a personal, family matter in which he was very much involved. I said that if he could fix it with the Transport Sergeant then that was entirely up to him but in no way could I be involved and, if he was caught, then I would have no knowledge of the matter so I would be unable to help him. He thanked me and said he fully understood this.

I was very intrigued by this request and it was not until some weeks later, when we were out of the line and having an officers/sergeants get-together that I found out the reason. Apparently, when we were in the Forlimpopoli area and the Troops were billeted in different farmhouses, Talbot's Troop was in a big farmhouse which had about 16 inhabitants ranging from great-grandfather down to great-grandchildren. It happened to be one of the Ities' birthdays so Talbot and his Troop decided it would be a good idea to have a party and got hold of plenty of vino and some hooch. It was in full swing when heavy thumping was heard upstairs and, on investigation, this turned out to be great-grandfather who wanted to know what all the noise was all about and, if it was a party, then he insisted on joining it. He was more or less bedridden so Talbot carried him downstairs to join the fun. He was having a great time when he suddenly keeled over, had a heart attack, and died on the spot (what a way to go!). The family burial plot was just on the outskirts of Forli, some way away, which was crawling with troops and, in particular, with Military Police. Talbot wanted a 3-ton lorry so that he could take great-grandfather, in his coffin, together with all the family in the back of the lorry to give the old boy a proper burial service in the family ground. Heaven knows what would have happened to him if the Military Police had stopped the lorry and unlashed the coverings on the back and found out what was inside. I found all this out at our Christmas party which we celebrated after we had pulled out of the line.

Somewhere about this time 'Ticker' Tilford MM, who was then my SQMS, celebrated two important things. Firstly, it was his 40th birthday and secondly, he was to be promoted to be my Squadron Sergeant-Major. He was taking over from SSM George DCM, a fine old Regular, who was going back to England on promotion and whose DCM was very well earned in the desert.

We were still near the sharp end and in a small and rather dilapidated farmhouse, but this was quite something to celebrate so he was asked to come up from the 'B' Echelon to have a drink with us.

He got well and truly plastered, we saw to that alright, and I had got hold of some candles, cut them in half, and stuck 40 of them on the stone floor, lit them, and he was told to blow them all out. As fast as he was doing this, we, rather unkindly, were of course re-lighting them and eventually when he was completely out of breath, and in the state he was, stood up unsteadily, took one look and said, "Oh shit!" and fell directly on them rolling about to extinguish the lot.

This didn't do his battle-dress much good so we pulled him off and gently took him outside and laid him in the back of his truck. As a final effort I removed the top of the iron stove in the room and draped it around his neck.

I understand that he was left to sleep it off in the back of his truck back in the Echelon and that when he woke up, eventually, he just couldn't make out where the hell he was or what had happened to him. He was black from head to foot and he thought that he had broken his neck as he couldn't move it and it was damn sore. He certainly wasn't around for about the next 48 hours.

The last of the German main defences were known as the Genghis Khan line which was based on the river Senio which was wide and steep with concrete banks. This line ran from the Appenine range of mountains, four or five miles to the west of Route 9, going east to Lake Comacchio about 20 miles further east. The whole area was completely criss-crossed with subsidiary little canals and behind the Genghis Khan line was the river Santerno which, ran from west to east from the mountains to Imola, on Route 9, which was about 15 miles south of Bologna, and the Santerno of course went into Lake Comacchio. The line, I suppose, was about eight to ten miles in depth with the usual dug-in infantry, mines, wire, machine-gun posts and anti-tank guns, and of course all roads and bridges were blown and mined and under observation.

Around about December 4th we were up in the rear of the forward area preparing to help elements of the 4th Indian Division to get across the river Senio and as the ground was completely and utterly waterlogged with all the main roads and bridges blown we sent working parties scouring the whole of the countryside to cut down small trees, to make fascines. These were bundles of young trees just over the width of the tank; there would be about 20 or 30 trees in a bundle and there three fascine bundles on each tank so that if we came to a blown road or bridge, like World War One when tanks had to cross trenches, we would come up to the blown holes and drop the fascines in them to make a wooden bridge so that we could get across. Strict orders were passed around that under no circumstances whatsoever were they to be used other than in actual active operations. A Court Martial offence if used unnecessarily.

'B' Squadron had 16 tanks in line ahead on a narrow dirt road which was about 15-20 feet above the surrounding sodden fields and with secondary roads at rightangles at the front and rear of us. We had orders to move up late in the afternoon, when it was getting dark, to the transverse road immediately in front of us and we had to be on that road at a certain time. I had been up on a recce to check the route and the time and had worked out that it would take us approximately 20 minutes to be at our rendezvous and I gave the order to start up and move accordingly.

The forward Troop started to move off and then it stopped and a runner came back from one of the tanks reporting that the road had collapsed in front of the leading tank, with a gap of 20 feet or more, so what were they to do? I then ordered the Squadron to go out in reverse to get onto the road behind us so that we could then belt up to our rendezvous. The rear tank started to reverse and it had only gone about 15-20 yards when exactly the same thing happened again - the bloody road collapsed with another 20 foot gap so there was the Squadron stuck with gaps fore and aft and unable to move. What the hell was I to do?

I judged it more important to get tanks up to the fighting area whether they had fascines or not so immediately gave the order that as many fascines as necessary would be used to plug the gap in front of the Squadron so that we could move forward. After some considerable time and difficulty this was done and fortunately the whole Squadron was able to move and get onto the road, but we were a good quarter of an hour late and there was absolute chaos and confusion going on all around us in the dark because other units were having the same sort of trouble. As it turned out we never had to use the fascines at all after that so it was a complete and utter waste of time and I shudder to think what the poor Italian farmers thought about the desecration of their trees.

As far as I can recollect the attack was not successful owing to the completely waterlogged ground and serious operations virtually ceased, for us at any rate, until about the first week in January when we did move back again, I think on the west side of Route 9, up into a bit more mountain country. 'C' and 'B' Squadrons were then manning one of the innumerable mountain ridges overlooking a road and a small tributary running from west to east. The sector here was very quiet except for the odd bit of shelling, if any movement was spotted, and an unusual decision was made here by RHQ who thought that it was unnecessary to have two complete Squadrons of tanks fully manned up there. So it was decided that 'C' Squadron tank personnel should leave their tanks up on the crest but pull back to enjoy Christmas whilst 'B' Squadron (of course it would be us) were told to stay up in strength to look after the whole group.

We were told to lie very doggo and not reveal ourselves and this was one occasion when I regret I completely disobeyed orders and turned a blind eye, or rather a deaf ear, to such instructions because one particular morning to my complete astonishment I saw a Panzer Mark IV going down the road on its own very slowly - quite what the hell it was doing I had no idea - I simply couldn't resist the opportunity and got Shapcott my gunner to lose off three quick rounds at it. His first shot was fractionally short, his second stopped it and appeared to break the tracks and the third obviously went into it, though it didn't brew-up.

I eventually reported back to RHQ and, to my disgust, got a rocket and was told under no circumstances was I to do that again without permission as we were meant to be lying doggo. Some time later that morning a lone RASC lorry was observed trundling along our side of the tributary and eventually wound its way up to where we were, raising a cloud of dust as it did so, and he was stopped by our chaps and brought along to me and I asked him what the hell he thought he was doing. He was a very young driver, and I would think new to the area, and he was totally lost and when I explained that he had been in full view of the enemy for about ten minutes and this was the extreme front edge of the sharp end the poor chap nearly fainted.

The next morning after our usual dawn stand-to, to my astonishment I observed a Nebelwerfer opening fire away down to our left flank. It must have been a mobile one and had moved right up to the top of the crest and I could see the flashes in the dark as it let fly with its five rockets, which it did three or four times. So I got on the radio and asked RHQ if I could have a crack at it and was emphatically told no, definitely not. I was very fed-up about this. Eventually 'C' Squadron came up to take over their tanks and we were told to pull out in the early hours of the morning, which was going to be quite a tricky operation because a little bit of shellfire had been coming down, as the enemy had obviously heard some movement in the area, and the only way that the Squadron could move out was to go down the track this young RASC driver had used, towards the enemy positions, then along the lateral road and then climb up back again round the rear of our ridge.

I was in a bit of a quandary whether to lead the Squadron out, or to be in the middle, or to be the last one out, and in the end I decided to be the last one out because I would have hated to have moved off and the rear half of the Squadron to have got into trouble and I wasn't there.

So somewhere around three or four am Johnnie Herbertson led the Squadron out and in the quiet of the dawn we seemed to be making one hell of a lot of noise and I was waiting for a real stonk to come down but thank God! it didn't except for a bit of shelling and some mortaring, but nothing really heavy. However I was very relieved indeed when we all finally pulled out and got back to our rest area. Here we were able to enjoy our belated Christmas festivities, at long last, somewhere around December 30th.

Once again, the troops of the Squadron were scattered around in different farmhouses so John and I decided to walk round all of them. Each Troop had got in a supply of Vino and hooch of all descriptions and it was a very hectic morning because each Troop tried to get us as plastered as possible in the shortest time possible. After visiting about the fourth Troop John then disappeared but I managed, somehow, to stagger round the whole Squadron before getting back to my farmhouse in a pretty chronic state. The farmhouse was a delightful place which, I believe, belonged to an Italian who had been an ardent admirer and supporter of Emily Pankhurst and the Suffragette Movement in World War One. Anyhow, I got up to my bedroom, feeling very much the worse for wear, and my batman suggested I went to bed but I insisted on being propped up against an open window and I completely passed out up there and I had my elbows wedged into the window. I was up there for about three hours and by the time my batman had come to see what had happened to me I was just about frozen stiff and I must have looked like one of the Foreign Legionnaires in Beau Geste when they were holding Fort Zinderneuf and all the dead men were put back up on the parapets, with a rifle sticking out in front of them, to give the Arabs the impression the Legionnaires were still alive and well. John, I am glad to say, recovered and carried on the session in the evening so honours were even.

During this time, when we were slowly inching our way up the Italian peninsula in the bitter cold of winter, we naturally billeted ourselves in whatever buildings we could find - farmhouses, cottages, etc.

It was not always possible to have a building which would take all the Squadron officers, seven of us, and often the Troop Leaders would be with their respective Troop - thus leaving myself at Squadron headquarters with John Herbertson.

I can remember many occasions when I would be on my own in the evening in some small room in a "Casa," writing either to my wife or bringing up-to-date the Squadron War Diary, by the dim light of a hurricane lamp or perhaps a gas-pressure lamp.

The door would open quietly and a bottle of gin would be placed gently, but firmly, on the table in front of me, followed by two glasses.

I would look up at John and with a sigh of resignation, or relief (?), finish or put away my writing and we would then get down to the business of demolishing the gin. (How he managed to get hold of it was not my business but he wasn't an ex-adjutant for nothing and a resourceful man was he.)

About two hours later we had put the world to right and discussed just about everything under the sun - little 'shop' except moaning, briefly, about the 'higher-paid-help,' and then happily to bed. (Happy memories my old friend...!)

In January/February we handed over our trusty Shermans for Churchills and our new CO, Pat Seaver DSO, ex-1st Army and a very fine bloke, had the three Squadron Commanders up and said, to my absolute horror, that one Squadron was to be equipped with flame-throwers. Having spent some months in hospital before the war with burns and having seen the horrendous effect during the war, I protested most bitterly at this and said that I would refuse to have a Squadron of that type and was prepared to resign my commission if I was ordered to do so. Pat laughed at this and said, "Don't be daft, you can't do that Ham, and I can't in fairness say that Hickey or Tom have got to have them because you don't want them. Will you agree we cut cards and see who has them?" and so reluctantly I agreed and of course I lost and I got the flame-throwing Squadron to my complete disgust. Thank God, and I mean that most sincerely, we never had to use the flame-throwers in action because the tank, in fact the main turret, still had the 75 millimetre and the flame-thrower was down in the front near the driver, and fortunately, by then, the war was nearly over.

In March we were attached to the Poles, our Regiment being attached to the 5th Battalion of the 2nd Carpathian Brigade of the 3rd Polish Division, who were extraordinarily fine blokes. Most of them had been in Eastern Poland and had therefore been overrun by the Russians, when the Russians moved in, and packed off to Siberia and then eventually when the Allies were so short of troops the Russians agreed for them to be released and they came down through Palestine and fought in the desert and then they came over to Italy. We trained hard with them and got to know them well as we were going to work with them in what was obviously going to be the final operation in Italy and it did appear, at long last, that the war was rapidly approaching an end with the news from the Russian front and of course from our own front with troops roaring into Germany.

We had a terrific liaison party with the Poles that 'B' Squadron was going to work with and our CO had impressed upon me and the other officers that under no circumstances were we to talk politics because this was a very dangerous subject. Somewhere around about one o'clock or two o'clock in the morning the acting Polish CO, who was a Captain or Major Dobrewicski, a small chap with a huge moustache and a large hook nose, and with tears streaming down his face, started to state his three pet hates. First of all it was the Germans and then the Russians and then Churchill, because the news had then come out that Churchill had agreed with the Russians that the division of Poland would be on the lines of the River Oder so his family's large estate and farms would thus be in Russian hands. I thought that this was getting to the point where we would have to get him to leave so I got hold of a ferocious drink of vodka, brandy and whisky mixed together and gave it to him. I had a similar looking drink, but nothing like so vicious, and got him to climb on top of a table with me, link arms and shouting out "Nostrovia" we downed our drinks in one gulp. I was waiting for him to pass out but damn it! we had to do this three or four times before he started to sway about, closing his eyes, and then totter over backwards! I was then able to say to his second in command, tactfully, "I think it's about time your CO went to bed, don't you?"

We then moved up forward into the battle area and on that morning I was at the HQ of the Polish infantry battalion with whom we were working. Their HQ was in a bombed-out house in the village and it was in such a precarious state that it looked as if it was about to collapse at any moment. To my horror the HQ was right down in the basement and as I am a rather claustrophobic character I was just petrified at having to go down there. It was airless and very hot so I took off the leather jacket I was wearing and to do this I had to undo my revolver belt and hung them both over the back of my chair.

Whilst we were discussing the forthcoming attack a message was passed to me saying that I was urgently required back at my own SHQ as there was the threat of a German tank counter-attack. I grabbed my jacket, rushed out to my Honey tank and roared back to the Squadron only to realise, half-way back, that I had forgotten to put on my revolver belt.

When I got back to the Squadron I found out that it was a complete flap after all so I turned round and hared back to the Polish HQ. Unfortunately they had moved on out by then and the old HQ had been taken over by a bunch of Partizani and, quite naturally, trying to find my revolver, belt, compass and ammunition pouch amongst that lot was totally hopeless. To cut a long story short, many weeks later I got another official OHMS envelope from some clerk up in the War Office again ticking me off for losing one revolver, 12 rounds of ammunition, one compass, to wit I would have to pay the sum of £5-12s-6d and consider myself lucky I wasn't on a Court Martial charge for losing a firearm.

Quoting from *The Tanks* by Captain Liddell Hart it states that:

> The terrain over which this last major battle in Italy was fought was flat and thickly cultivated with vines which restricted both vision and movement on the roads. Small villages and individual farmhouses were dotted about, each one a potential stronghold. The rivers of which there were many ran from south west to north east right across the line of

advance. Between the rivers the land was a maze of streams, canals and irrigation ditches. The majority of the larger canals and rivers had high flood banks on each side which formed suitable obstacles to vehicles. The river Po was a wide swift running river and could not be crossed without major bridging or rafting operations.

The river Senio over which the initial assault had to be made was a narrow but deep stream with flood banks 30 feet high. The enemy had fortified the far bank very strongly and in places still held the near flood bank which was heavily mined. At each crossing place selected for the armour it was necessary with detachments from the 25th Armoured Assault Brigade to blow a hole through the flooded bank of the nearside, bulldoze a passage, put one or more bridge tanks into the river, blast a hole in the opposite bank, and get a bulldozer over to make a passage before the fighting tanks could cross.

The crossings of the Senio on the Polish Corps front were so hotly opposed that, after 24 hours delay, some of the tanks allotted to co-operate with it had to be sent across by Bailey Bridge thrown across over on a New Zealand Division sector further north. The 6th RTR then went across the Lugo canal south of that town whilst the 8th RTR on its left assisted the Polish Infantry in the capture of Solarolo and both then reached the Santurno river on April 11th and crossed it to bring much needed help to the Infantry hard pressed on the further banks.

The attack was due to start on the early morning of April 9th and as April 10th was my wedding anniversary (our fourth) I wrote to my wife saying that by the time she got that letter I would be in it once more and apparently this was the only time she ever broke down. She had been so brave and so strong for so long that it seemed so unfair to her that, after four long years, I was still abroad and still in action when so many of her friends, and husbands of friends, had been abroad for a much shorter period and had come back - but that's how it was.

I was with the Polish infantry HQ and had a briefing the night before and gone to bed fairly late when I was suddenly wakened, about 5.30am by the Polish Intelligence Officer. He could speak pretty good English and was shaking my shoulder vigorously and saying, "Major! Wake up. Major! Wake up quickly!" I sat up with a jerk and exclaimed, "Christ! What's happened? Has there been a Jerry counter-attack? What the hell's gone wrong?" "Nothing wrong" he said "Great day! Great day! It's my birthday! Here drink this!" and he gave me a tumbler full of neat brandy which of course I had to drink. Those bloody Poles! They were a bloody menace.

The attack went well because the 8th Army had been preparing for this all through the winter and the Germans by now were getting somewhat demoralised and just hadn't got the stomach for any more hard fighting so it was just a question of pushing on as far and as fast as possible. When we came up to Solarolo the infantry were beginning to lag behind quite a bit, I think, to do a bit of personal looting in the various houses, so I suggested to the Polish Brigadier Rudniki that he should come with me in my Honey tank, which had good wireless communications, which would give him much better control and that he should put as many as possible of the infantry on the backs of our tanks so that we could then press on hard.

If and when we came up against any opposition we would blast it with our 75mm's and machine-guns and the Poles could jump off and go in with our fire support. He thought that this was a tremendous idea and agreed to it and the advance went forward very fast indeed after that.

On April 11th we reached and crossed the Santurno river and on April 15th we had gone through Imola which was little more than 15 miles south of Bologna. By April 17/18th we were in Castel Maggiore and on April 19th we were on the Bologna-Ferrara road, east of Bologna, and on April 21st Bologna itself was liberated. Johnnie Herbertson and I somehow managed to roar into town in our jeep and I think that we must have been just about the first British officers to get into Bologna and a great time was had by us and the deliriously happy townspeople.

The campaign in Italy was now virtually over as the Germans were just pulling back everywhere and offering little resistance and surrendering in large numbers.

Finally the almost unbelievable happened - something for which we had been hoping and praying for so very long.

On May 2nd came the simply incredible and absolutely marvellous news that the Germans had surrendered in Italy - six days before they surrendered completely in Germany itself on May 8th.

We were then north and east of Bologna I think somewhere in the region of Minerbio, and it is strange that I cannot remember the name of the actual place on such a momentous day. When the news finally came through - it was absolutely stupendous and almost impossible to take in - I got hold of our jeep and all the Squadron officers piled in and we roared off to the little town to spread the glad tidings.

There were hundreds of Italians about and they all knew that something was happening and I drove in through shouting crowds with the headlights blazing, horn blowing and all of us shouting and waving like mad. We drove into a rather lovely little piazza which had long, narrow, horizontal steps leading up to a pink fountain in the centre and, theatrically, I drove the jeep up the steps and did a crash-stop by the fountain.

I jumped out onto the bonnet and in my excruciating English/Italian bellowed out that the war was over; that the Germans had surrendered; the war had ended. For a moment there was a stunned silence so I yelled out again, "Tedeschi Kaput! La Guerra Finita Touta Italia! Armistice! La Guerra Finita Officiale! Viva Ingelaise! Viva! Viva!" There was then a great roar of cheering and shouting that went up and in their hundreds they came running towards the jeep, waving flags, shouting, cheering, weeping. It was terrific.

Suddenly there was the staccato burst of automatic gun-fire and people started screaming with fright and horror, throwing themselves on the ground or turning and running back. The fountain beside the jeep erupted, the windscreen shattered and Eric Broadfoot, one of my Troop Leaders who was a South African, cried out and fell down with blood streaming down one of his legs. It was mind-numbingly chaotic.

"Good God Almighty!" I thought, "What the hell's this? A last ditch stand? A last ditch fanatic? Where, what the hell...?" and then I suddenly saw him and yelled, "There he is? Get him!" It wasn't a German or a Fascisti - it was a very drunken and excited Partizani with a red, green and white scarf round his neck and he was firing his automatic rifle up in the air. He then noticed the fountain and lowering his rifle was hose-piping it with short sweeps and that's why the bullets were pinging just everywhere.

With a great shout we all jumped out of the jeep and grabbed him and someone got hold of his rifle, tearing it out of his hands and smashed the barrel on the ground and bent it. We then hoisted him up, gave a great heave and chucked him into the fountain.

David Hotham, an Old Etonian, and a great friend of Eric also jumped in and sat astride him, lifting the Partizani's head up and kept bashing it down again. He was using the most frightful language and blood and broken teeth were coming up. I yelled out, "For Christ's sake David - you're drowning the poor bastard - get off him - get off you idiot!" I simply dare not repeat what David was saying.

It really was incredible to think that this drunken lunatic, at the very moment of triumph and victory, could have caused many casualties and worse, could easily have killed or wounded us. It was really the most extraordinary ending to the war! Anybody who had been more than two years abroad was then flown back to England and that's when I left the 8th Tanks. They eventually returned to the UK and went up to Thetford in Norfolk, I think, ready to do training and go out to the Far East, but Thank God the Japanese surrendered before that was necessary.

I think it might be of interest here to list decorations awarded to the Regiment:-

	Regiment	'B' Squadron
DSO	6	1
MC	18	6
MBE	2	1
DCM	1	1
MM	25	10
BEM	2	nil
TOTAL:	54	19

Many more awards should have been made as many people were recommended but for some reason or another did not get one. However I think that the brief narratives regarding the Western Desert Campaign and the Italian Campaign, together with the above table, show that the men of the 8th Battalion of the Royal Tank Regiment lived up to the highest standard and tradition of the Royal Tank Corps and the Regimental motto: Fear Naught.

I, for one, am very proud indeed to have had the privilege and the honour of serving with such a fine body of men.

I have already mentioned two rather remarkable coincidences, the first of which concerned by brother and I when we flew back to the UK from Italy after the war ended. We flew back on the same day, in the same flight and landed at Peterborough aerodrome. We then telephoned, from the same telephone box, our mother and wives to say that we were safely back home.

The second one was when my wife and I were on holiday in Italy, in May 1968, and doing a tour of the Gothic Line battle area. We found a cemetery at Coriano, which I didn't even know was there and when my wife took a final look back as we were leaving she found the grave of my driver L/Cpl Tim Clayton, who had died in my arms on that ridge 24 years earlier in 1944.

The third one is every bit as extraordinary. When we left the UK in April 1941 to go out to the ME our convoy had five Merchant ships carrying munitions and supplies, including our Matilda tanks, for Malta and the ME. At Gibraltar they left us and headed off for the passage to Malta and Alexandria through the Mediterranean with a strong naval escort - whilst we went on round the Cape of Good Hope and up to Suez.

They were heavily attacked by air, surface ships and submarines and the ship with our tanks on board, carrying skeleton crews which included my driver, John Bainbridge, was torpedoed and sunk. Whilst he was in the water the ship exploded and as she went down he saw a tank cartwheel into the air and crash down on the deck of a naval ship coming to their rescue. He told me that he would always be grateful to the Navy for their sterling work and the way they treated those they picked up. The ship was HMS *Naiad*.

When I came to live in Shaftesbury in 1986 I joined their Probus Club, also a nearby golf club, and a good friend of mine now is Lt. Cmdr. Vince Carey, DSM RN Retd., who is a fellow member of both clubs. He was a CPO Engineer on board HMS *Naiad* that day so his ship, some 51 years ago, rescued not just an army bloke; not just a tank crew bloke; his ship rescued my own tank driver.

I think that is stretching 'the long arm of coincidence' somewhat as we are all alive today and, dare I say it once more, "Truth is stranger than fiction."

Was it all worthwhile?

As an old man of 75 I can only leave that to history to judge but to the memory of so many fine men who died and suffered in the Desert and in Italy - far too many - I would like to quote the inscription on the memorial erected to the 14th Army men after the battles of Kohima and Imphal. That inscription reads:

> When you go home
> tell them of us and say
> for their tomorrow
> we gave our today

MILITARY CROSS AWARD

LIEUT. S.G. HAMILTON
8th Bn RTR

28th May 1942 Point 187
3rd June 1942 Eleut Et Tamar

This Officer in many previous actions has shown conspicuous gallantry and disregard for danger and at all times has been an outstanding example to his men.

At Point 187 on 28th May 1942, whilst with 'Stopcol', when his Squadron was attacked by an overwhelming number of tanks and his Squadron Commander was wounded, he not only showed conspicuous gallantry by rescuing his Squadron Commander in the face of heavy fire, but quickly took control of the Squadron himself.

On the evening of 3rd June 1942 at Eleut Et Tamar it was almost entirely due to his gallantry and determination to hold the position that prevented our guns from being overrun by no less than 60 tanks that outflanked them.

POLISH CROSS OF VALOUR AWARD

In April 1945 after the attack with the Polish 3rd Carpathian Brigade near Bologna the author was recommended for the Cross of Valour, the Polish equivalent of the Military Cross. But he then went on leave and never received the medal. A chance remark to a Polish friend in about 1980 resulted in the award finally being notified in the *London Gazette* of 21/9/1983 and in November of that year the award was presented by General Rudnicki, who commanded the Poles in the attack, at the Polish Institute and General Sikorski Museum in London.

THE ROYAL TANK REGIMENT

PERSONAL MESSAGE FROM
FIELD-MARSHAL MONTGOMERY

1. Having been appointed by His Majesty The King to be a Colonel Commandant of the Royal Tank Regiment, I should like at once to send my personal greetings to all officers, warrant officers, NCOs and men of the Regiment.

2. It is a great honour for me to be given this appointment. My connections with the R.T.R. have been very close since the days of Alamein: during which battle I was given your beret and your badge by a Sgt. in the Regiment who commanded my tank. I have proudly worn your beret and your badge ever since that day.

3. I have served with many units of the Regiment throughout the war years. From my own experience in this war I can say that The Royal Tank Regiment has carried on with much distinction the great traditions which were so deservedly won in the Great War of 1914/18; its units have fought magnificently in every theatre.

4. During the last six years battalions of the Regiment have been called upon to serve in every type of armoured formation, and with every type of tank and specialised equipment. But whatever has been their task, they have carried it through with distinction. The Regiment has made a great name for itself. Let us see that that name flourishes in the years that lie ahead.

5. I have met many of you from time to time. I look forward to meeting you again in due course. You can rest assured that I will serve the Regiment to the best of my ability, and will endeavour always to promote its interests.

6. Good luck to you all.

B. L. Montgomery

Germany

Sept, 1945.

Field-Marshal,

Colonel Commandant, The R.T.R.

ALLIED FORCE HEADQUARTERS

2 May, 1945

SPECIAL ORDER OF· THE DAY

Soldiers, Sailors and Airmen of the Allied Forces in the Mediterranean Theatre

After nearly two years of hard and continuous fighting which started in Sicily in the summer of 1943, you stand today as the victors of the Italian Campaign.

You have won a victory which has ended in the complete and utter rout of the German armed forces in the Mediterranean. By clearing Italy of the last Nazi aggressor, you have liberated a country of over 40,000,000 people.

Today the remnants of a once proud Army have laid down their arms to you—close on a million men with all their arms, equipment and impedimenta.

You may well be proud of this great and victorious campaign which will long live in history as one of the greatest and most successful ever waged.

No praise is high enough for you sailors, soldiers, airmen and workers of the United Forces in Italy for your magnificent triumph.

My gratitude to you and my admiration is unbounded and only equalled by the pride which is mine in being your Commander-in-Chief.

H. R. Alexander

Field-Marshal,
Supreme Allied Commander,
Mediterranean Theatre.

Roll of Honour

	Date of death	Cemetery or Memorial
7933564 L/Cpl. John Ackley	19/9/44	Cassino Memorial
6011253 Tpr. Vincent W. Adams	5/6/42	Knightsbridge
7888757 Sgt. John F. Allan	31/10/42	Tripoli
87440 Lt. John H. Anderson (HQ)	7/12/41	Halfaya
7937157 Tpr. Cyril R. Anderson (C)	4/11/42	Alamein
3458637 Tpr. George A. Atherton	25/9/44	Ancona
7911335 Tpr. Louis Baker	8/12/41	Knightsbridge
162152 Capt. Maurice Ball	5/6/42	Alamein Memorial
7888893 Cpl. Walter Barnes MM	10/9/44	Cassino Memorial
7884168 Sgt. Edward Barnett MM (C)	10/5/42	Alamein Memorial
Capt. R. Batten MC, MiD (A)	9/44	Gradara
7942787 Tpr. Maurice Beadle	19/9/44	Ancona
7910966 Tpr. Douglas G. Beaton	8/7/42	Alamein
557207 Sgt. Victor Beeton	1/7/42	Alamein Memorial
7888417 Sgt. Kenneth G. Beavers (B)	14/9/44	Coriano
7918970 Tpr. Derrick H. Berry (C)	3/11/42	Alamein
7885088 Sgt. Ernest S. Blackwell	12/12/41	Alexandria
7911341 Cpl. John G. Bower	2/9/44	Gradara
7886920 Cpl. John E. Boynton	6/9/44	Montecchio
7943279 Tpr. Thomas L. Brett	16/7/42	Alamein
7925804 Tpr. Edwin W. Broadley	19/9/44	Cassino Memorial
7888755 Tpr. Thomas Brown	31/10/42	Alamein
7889067 Sgt. Matthew Buist	6/9/44	Gradara
7890058 Tpr. Frederick G. Burlingham	29/11/41	Halfaya
74913 Major Peter J. D. E. Butt (B)	14/9/44	Gradara
7911345 Tpr. Patrick F. Caffery	29/11/41	Knightsbridge
176697 2/Lt. Frank A. H. Cash (A)	29/11/41	Halfaya
170277 2/Lt. John A. Chapman (C)	10/7/42	Alamein
877801 Tpr. Edward Cheeseman	19/9/44	Coriano
321231 L/Cpl. Sydney Clayton (B)	7/10/44	Coriano
7911352 L/Cpl. Albert S. Clayton	29/11/41	Halfaya
7879038 Cpl. Frederick T. Clee (B)	7/6/42	Knightsbridge
7912667 Tpr. Joseph Coates	8/9/44	Ancona
197968 Lt. Cedric T. Cooke (C)	6/11/42	Alamein
7887264 Tpr. Denis Connor	9/2/45	Forli
7888931 Tpr. Alastair Cormack (B)	26/11/41	Knightsbridge
7918061 Tpr. Frank L. Cotton (C)	23/11/41	Knightsbridge
7888777 Tpr. Alfred G. Crompton	10/5/42	At sea

7894238 Tpr. John T. Cronin	6/11/42	Heliopolis
7914157 Tpr. Harold Crowley	3/12/41	Alamein Memorial
7926985 Tpr. Frederick S. Cryer	3/11/42	Alamein
102319 Lt. Denis A. W. Davis (C)	23/11/41	Knightsbridge
7886336 Tpr. Edward J. Daysh (C)	3/11/42	Alamein Memorial
7922466 Tpr. John Deakin	4/12/41	Alamein Memorial
7919120 Tpr. David C. Dunbar	3/11/42	Alamein Memorial
7918908 L/Sgt. Albert B. Dunce	3/11/42	Alamein Memorial
7933506 Tpr. James R. Ellis	6/9/44	Montecchio
7940302 Tpr. James Ellwood	14/9/44	Coriano
7889242 Tpr. David T. Evans	4/12/43	Ancona (p.o.w.)
160181 Lt. William. H. Fairclough MC (A)	3/11/42	Alamein
7925809 Tpr. Rowland Farlie	31/10/42	Alamein
7925811 Tpr. John R. Fenn	27/11/41	Halfaya
7904060 Tpr. George Fenney (C)	21/9/44	Gradara
7952037 Tpr. Robert Findlay	19/9/44	Cassino
7888684 Tpr. George R. Frost	5/6/42	Tobruk
7889095 Tpr. Alfred Fry	5/6/42	Alamein Memorial
7925816 Tpr. Reginald N. Golding	3/11/42	Alamein Memorial
7885543 Cpl. John Graves (C)	17/12/41	Heliopolis
6943026 L/Cpl. Arthur R. Gravener	20/1/43	Caserta (p.o.w.)
7889098 Cpl. James Greener	8/12/41	Knightsbridge
7920589 Tpr. Douglas G. Grimes (C)	9/7/42	Alamein
5124632 Tpr. Norman A. Ham	19/9/44	Cassino Memorial
7880153 Sgt. Edward Handley	29/11/41	Knightsbridge
7919057 L/Cpl. Norman Hilton (C)	8/9/44	Gradara
7882295 Tpr. Alan D. Howcroft (C)	21/12/44	Faenza
Lt. H. C. (Mike) Hunt MiD	9/42	Alamein
7912481 Tpr. Harold S. Jarratt (C)	23/11/41	Knightsbridge
7888994 L/Cpl. Amrose W. Johnson (C)	27/5/42	Alamein Memorial
7924842 Tpr. George E. A. Jones	8/12/41	Knightsbridge
7944470 Tpr. James M. Kerr	14/6/44	Sangro River
7921388 Tpr. Edward H. Kilkenny (C)	1/12/41	Knightsbridge
124524 Capt. Peter R. Kitto MiD (C)	8/12/42	(in Palestine)
7890059 L/Cpl. Ronald E. Lain	3/11/42	Alamein
7936869 Tpr. Thomas H. Law	5/9/45	Caserta
7904450 Tpr. James L. Lee	24/11/41	Halfaya
7888918 Cpl. Arthur W. Lenton	16/4/45	Forli
7918145 Tpr. John Lorimer (C)	31/12/41	Halfaya
7919002 Tpr. William J. Mallen (C)	23/11/41	Knightsbridge
7889657 Tpr. Michael W. J. McBean (B)	16/7/42	Alamein Memorial
7909673 Tpr. Edgar F. W. Nash	2/11/42	Alamein
7885509 Sgt. Walter F. Nendick (B)	5/12/41	Alamein Memorial

130256 Capt. John Newman (B)	25/9/44	Gradara
32630 Major John A. O'Neill (A)	29/11/41	Knightsbridge
7911042 Tpr. Wilfred E. Orton	28/11/41	Knoghtsbridge
7902256 Tpr. Edwin Parden (B)	23/6/44	Caserta
36593 Cpl. George M. Parr	3/11/42	Alamein Memorial
7917834 Tpr. Bernard L. Patrick	29/11/41	Alamein Memorial
7929687 Tpr. Walter Patrick	14/12/41	Alamein Memorial
150565 Cpl. Benjamin G. Pearce	19/9/44	Coriano
7877479 Tpr. Robert Pemberton	20/12/43	Alexandria
4617523 Tpr. Leslie Pickering (B)	6/9/44	Coriano
7916385 Tpr. Frank Piper	4/12/41	Alamein Memorial
14505507 Tpr. George Raybould	13/10/44	Cesena
128793 2/Lt. Roland A. Reed (C)	31/12/41	Halfaya
259277 Lt. Frederick Roberts MM	14/9/44	Coriano
Sgt. Roberts (B)	11/41	(Sidi Rezegh)
3459344 Tpr. Kenneth Scott	1/9/44	Gradara
7942895 Tpr. Thomas Shillington (C)	3/11/42	Alamein Memorial
7888392 Tpr. George A. V. Simmons	29/11/41	Alamein Memorial
7878932 Cpl. David R. Sims	16/7/42	Alamein
7886735 L/Cpl. Arthur Smith (B)	24/11/41	Halfaya
7888930 Cpl. Jack Smith	6/9/44	Coriano
7899889 Tpr. Robert J. Smith	8/6/44	Sangro River
7886330 Tpr. Richard E. Stammer	29/11/41	Knightsbridge
7908383 L/Sgt. Jo F. C. Sterne	14/9/44	Gradara
7888718 Sgt. Francis E. Steward	18/4/45	Coriano
Lt. L. J. Stock (B)	11/4/44	(Egypt)
3321813 Tpr. Walter P. Taylor	14/9/44	(Egypt)
7911408 Tpr. Joseph P. Taylor	8/9/44	(Egypt)
130260 Lt. Ian B. V. S. Taylor	23/11/41	Knightsbridge
7885610 Sgt. Pryce Thomas	28/11/41	Knightsbridge
7879617 Sgt. Ronald T. Thompson	23/11/41	Alamein Memorial
166178 2/Lt. Peter H. Thornely	29/11/41	Alamein Memorial
7888992 Tpr. Victor T. Thorpe	2/9/44	Montecchio
7904776 Tpr. Rowland Timberlake	1/7/42	Alamein Memorial
7880005 L/Cpl. John W. Tomlinson	21/12/44	Forli
Lt. W. Towers (A)	9/44	Coriano
7935159 Tpr. John Walker	6/9/44	Coriano
5181809 Tpr. Isaac Williams	11/4/45	Faenza
7899648 Tpr. Derrick C. Wood	24/11/41	Alamein Memorial
307793 Lt. Frederick H. R. Wood	13/9/44	Gradara
7887116 Cpl. William C. Worth	24/11/41	Alamein Memorial
7948338 Cpl. Robert D. Wright	6/8/45	Rome

Awards

Distinguished Service Order

Lt. Col. J. G. S. Compton	14/11/43
Major T. E. Hendrie	8/2/45
Lt. Col. G. E. Knox-Peebles	24/2/45
Major F. R. Lindsey MC	24/9/42
Lt. Col. S. D. W. Seaver	13/12/45
Major G. F. S. Sutton MC	24/9/42

Bar to Military Cross

Major B. F. McCabe	18/2/43
Major H. G. Sugden	15/10/42
Major G. F. S. Sutton DSO, MC	9/9/42 (Cross awarded 1918)

Military Cross

Lt. E. L. Allsup	8/3/45
Lt. R. C. Batten	31/12/42
Lt. R. J. Campbell	1942
2/Lt. B. Carter	24/9/42
Lt. I. S. Gray OBE, TD	13/12/42
Lt. P. C. Gunter	8/2/45
Lt. S. G. Hamilton	24/9/42
Capt. F. R. Lindsay	24/2/42
Capt. B. F. McCabe	9.9.42
Lt. I. MacDonald	23/8/45
Lt. G. H. Sugden	9/9/42
Capt. J. C. Robinson	1944
Major P. N. Veale	24/9/42

Member of the Order of the British Empire

Capt. J. R. Herbertson TD	1944
Major P. Hordern	1944

British Empire Medal

Sgt. E. E. Clarke	18/2/43
Sgt. E. S. Hickin	13/12/45

Distinguished Conduct Medal

Sgt. I. L. George	9/9/42

Bar to Military Medal

L/Cpl. D. Adams	8/2/45
Sgt. D. Condon	8/2/45

Military Medal

L/Cpl. D. Adams	25/9/42
L/Cpl. W. Barnes	24/9/44
Sgt. E. Barnett	24/2/42
Cpl. A. Bulloch	24/9/42
Tpr. D. Condon	24/9/42
SQMS S. Davies	13/12/45
Tpr. F. Daykin	24/9/42
Sgt. M. J. Elliott	24/9/42
Cpl. H. W. Haines	9/9/42
SQMS F. H. Johnson	13/12/45
Tpr. W. H. Knox	5/11/42
Sgt. J. W. Lambert	26/6/45
SQMS E. Lawrie	8/2/43
Tpr. R. J. Locke	24/2/42
Sgt. A. E. Mavers	31/12/42
Cpl. H. Moore	18/2/43
L/Cpl. Pine	1943
L/Cpl. J. B. Roberts	12/5/42
Sgt. A. H. Simpkins	19/3/42
L/Cpl. H. Stretton	31/12/42
Sgt. A. E. Tilford	18/12/43
Sgt. L. Wakefield	9/9/42

American Bronze Star

Capt. J. R. Herbertson MBE, TD   23/5/47

Polish Virtuti Militari 3rd Class

Lt. Col. S. D. W. WeaverDSO   1945

Polish Cross of Valour

Major S. G. Hamilton MC   awarded April 1945,
                                           Gazetted 21/9/83

Mention in Despatches
(regrettably this list is incomplete)

Lt. R. Batten MC
Lt. Col. F. K. Brooke
Capt. R. J. Campbell MC (twice)
Major S. G. Hamilton MC
Major T. E. Hendrie DSO
Lt. H. C. (Mike) Hunt
Lt. P. R. Kitto
Major J. J. O'Neill
Major G. E. Knox-Peebles DSO
Lt. Col. S. D. W. Weaver DSO (twice)
Major G. H. Sugden MC (twice)
Major J. A. Tildesley
Major P. N. Veale MC
Lt. Col. J. L. Winberg

WO J. Gwilliam
WO A. Parry
Sgt. M. J. Elliott MM
Sgt. C. E. Freeman
Sgt. C. Nunnington
Sgt. A. W. Simpkins MM
Sgt. J. Vockins
L/Cpl. D. Adams MM

Index